Am I Okay?
Psychological Testing and What Those Tests Mean

Anorexia Nervosa:
Starving for Attention

Child Abuse and Neglect:
Examining the Psychological Components

Conduct Unbecoming:
Hyperactivity, Attention Deficit, and Disruptive Behavior Disorders

Cutting the Pain Away:
Understanding Self-Mutilation

Disorders First Diagnosed in Childhood

Drowning Our Sorrows:
Psychological Effects of Alcohol Abuse

Life Out of Focus:
Alzheimer's Disease and Related Disorders

The Mental Effects of Heroin

Mental Illness and Its Effect on School and Work Environments

Out of Control:
Gambling and Other Impulse Control Disorders

Personality Disorders

Psychological Disorders Related to Designer Drugs

■ **Psychological Effects of Cocaine and Crack Addiction**

■ **Schizophrenia:**
Losing Touch with Reality

■ **Sexual Disorders**

■ **Sibling Rivalry:**
Relational Problems Involving Brothers and Sisters

■ **Sleep Disorders**

■ **Smoke Screen:**
Psychological Disorders Related to Nicotine Use

■ **Strange Visions:**
Hallucinogen-Related Disorders

■ **Through a Glass Darkly:**
The Psychological Effects of Marijuana and Hashish

■ **The Tortured Mind:**
The Many Faces of Manic Depression

■ **Uneasy Lives:**
Understanding Anxiety Disorders

■ **When Families Fail:**
Psychological Disorders and Dysfunctional Families

■ **A World Upside Down and Backwards:**
Reading and Learning Disorders

THE ENCYCLOPEDIA OF PSYCHOLOGICAL DISORDERS

Senior Consulting Editor Carol C. Nadelson, M.D.
Consulting Editor Claire E. Reinburg

PERSONALITY DISORDERS

Linda Bayer, Ph.D.

CHELSEA HOUSE PUBLISHERS
Philadelphia

The author dedicates this book to Eli Rosenbaum, whose devotion to justice in both public and private life is a treasure to us all. As lead prosecutor of Nazi murderers for the Justice Department, as well as an outstanding author and community leader, Eli embodies a commitment to righteousness and a passion for humanity that are two sides of the same coin. History evinces so few who are so wise.

The ENCYCLOPEDIA OF PSYCHOLOGICAL DISORDERS provides up-to-date information on the history of, causes and effects of, and treatment and therapies for problems affecting the human mind. The titles in this series are not intended to take the place of the professional advice of a psychiatrist or mental health care professional.

Chelsea House Publishers
Editor in Chief: Stephen Reginald
Production Manager: Pamela Loos
Art Director: Sara Davis
Director of Photography: Judy L. Hasday
Managing Editor: James D. Gallagher

Staff for PERSONALITY DISORDERS
Prepared by P. M. Gordon Associates, Philadelphia
Picture Researcher: Gillian Speeth, Picture This
Associate Art Director: Takeshi Takahashi
Cover Designer: Emiliano Begnardi

The Chelsea House World Wide Website address is
http://www.chelseahouse.com

First Printing

9 8 7 6 5 4 3 2

Library of Congress Cataloging-in-Publication Data

Bayer, Linda N.

Personality disorders / by Linda Bayer.
p. cm. — (Encyclopedia of psychological disorders)
Includes bibliographical references (p.) and index.
ISBN 0-7910-5317-2 (hc.)
1. Personality disorders. I. Title. II. Series.
RC554.B39 2000
616.89—dc21   99-28888
                                              CIP

CONTENTS

Introduction by Carol C. Nadelson, M.D.   6

Personality Disorders: An Overview   9

1   What Are Personality Disorders?   11

2   Paranoid Personality Disorder   19

3   Schizoid and Schizotypal Personality Disorders   27

4   Antisocial Personality Disorder   35

5   Borderline Personality Disorder   45

6   Histrionic and Narcissistic Personality Disorders   55

7   Avoidant and Dependent Personality Disorders   67

8   Obsessive-Compulsive Personality Disorder   75

Appendix: For More Information   84

Bibliography   85

Further Reading   88

Glossary   89

Index   91

PSYCHOLOGICAL DISORDERS AND THEIR EFFECT

CAROL C. NADELSON, M.D.
PRESIDENT AND CHIEF EXECUTIVE OFFICER,
The American Psychiatric Press

There are a wide range of problems that are considered psychological disorders, including mental and emotional disorders, problems related to alcohol and drug abuse, and some diseases that cause both emotional and physical symptoms. Psychological disorders often begin in early childhood, but during adolescence we see a sharp increase in the number of people affected by these disorders. It has been estimated that about 20 percent of the U.S. population will have some form of mental disorder sometime during their lifetime. Some psychological disorders appear following severe stress or trauma. Others appear to occur more often in some families and may have a genetic or inherited component. Still other disorders do not seem to be connected to any cause we can yet identify. There has been a great deal of attention paid to learning about the causes and treatments of these disorders, and exciting new research has taught us a great deal in the past few decades.

The fact that many new and successful treatments are available makes it especially important that we reject old prejudices and outmoded ideas that consider mental disorders to be untreatable. If psychological problems are identified early, it is possible to prevent serious consequences. We should not keep these problems hidden or feel shame that we or a member of our family has a mental disorder. Some people believe that something they said or did caused a mental disorder. Some people think that these disorders are "only in your head" so that you could "snap out of it" if you made the effort. This type of thinking implies that a treatment is a matter of willpower or motivation. It is a terrible burden for someone who is suffering to be blamed for his or her misery, and often people with psychological disorders are not treated compassionately. We hope that the information in this book will teach you about various mental illnesses.

The problems covered in the volumes of the ENCYCLOPEDIA OF PSYCHOLOGICAL DISORDERS were selected because they are of particular importance to young adults, because they affect them directly or because they affect family and friends. There are individual volumes on reading disorders, attention deficit and disruptive behavior disorders, and dementia—all of these are related to our abilities to learn and integrate information from the world around us. There are books on drug abuse that provide useful information about the effects of these drugs and treatments that are available for those individuals who have drug problems. Some of the books concentrate on one of the most common mental disorders, depression. Others deal with eating disorders, which are dangerous illnesses that affect a large number of young adults, especially women.

Most of the public attention paid to these disorders arises from a particular incident involving a celebrity that awakens us to our own vulnerability to psychological problems. These incidents of celebrities or public figures revealing their own psychological problems can also enable us to think about what we can do to prevent and treat these types of problems.

"Personality" is the name we give to the patterns of thinking, feeling, and behaving that one person exhibits consistently over time. When personality traits cause a person distress or interfere with his or her ability to function in society, the person is said to have a personality disorder.

PERSONALITY DISORDERS: AN OVERVIEW

When we refer to someone's *personality,* we're usually talking about a fundamental aspect of identity. So what does it mean to say that someone has a *personality disorder?* How can something so basic be disordered?

Some people have personality traits—that is, long-term and pervasive patterns of thinking, feeling, or behaving—that are very different from what their culture expects. That in itself is not a disorder. But if these traits cause the person a lot of distress or significantly disturb his or her ability to function in the world, a psychiatrist may diagnose a personality disorder.

Today, personality disorders are divided into ten types: paranoid, schizoid, schizotypal, antisocial, borderline, histrionic, narcissistic, avoidant, dependent, and obsessive-compulsive. Although some symptoms appear in more than one category, the ten types differ greatly from one another. One individual with a personality disorder may be extremely inhibited in any social setting. Another may aggressively demand attention or interfere with the rights of others.

No one "cause" has been identified for personality disorders. Heredity—the biological predisposition inherited from one's parents—generally seems to play a part, but so do a person's experiences, especially during childhood and adolescence. Similarly, no one treatment works for all personality disorders. Patients usually receive some form of psychotherapy ("talk" therapy), and a large percentage receive medication as well. Although the success of treatment varies, many individuals with personality disorders can learn to function well in everyday life.

Enlivened by vivid examples, this volume of the ENCYCLOPEDIA OF PSYCHOLOGICAL DISORDERS explores the wide variety of conditions that are found among the ten categories of personality disorders.

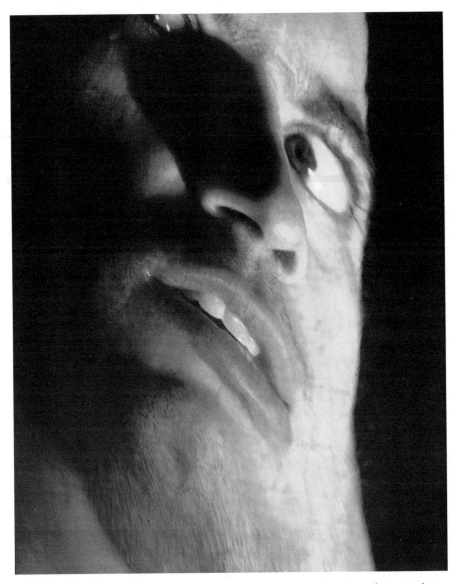

Though personality may be molded by many things at different times, it tends to remain stable over the course of a person's life. Similarly, most personality disorders are slow to change without medical intervention. Psychologists have identified ten broad categories of personality disorder.

1

PARANOID PERSONALITY DISORDER

The term *personality disorders* applies to a broad group of psychological conditions. Most psychologists recognize 10 different disorders as belonging to this group. To understand why so many conditions are placed in one category, we have to look at the basic concept of *personality*.

Your personality is made up of your enduring patterns of perceiving, relating to, and thinking about your environment and yourself. Essentially, it is the particular set of thoughts, feelings, and behaviors that makes you who you are—the sum total of your mental and emotional qualities and traits. As such, it is relatively stable. In five years you may radically revise your opinion of the current U.S. president, but your personality is not likely to change so fast.

Sigmund Freud, the father of psychoanalysis, believed that personality was pretty well set by the end of the first few years of life. A sense of basic trust, for example, begins in infancy when a baby learns that his or her needs are met and the world is essentially safe—or not.

Other theorists, however, have stressed the ways in which personality can be shaped in later stages of life, including adolescence and early adulthood. This means that although our personalities may be stable, they are not absolutely fixed. For many of us, the development of personality is a lifelong process.

Personality is affected by both hereditary and environmental factors. Heredity involves the traits a person inherits biologically from his or her parents. Just as people can inherit tendencies to be tall or short, lean or chubby, they can inherit elements of their personalities—and, sometimes, a predisposition to a particular type of personality disorder. Environment, however, also has an enormous impact. Your upbringing, your early experiences, your later achievements and disappointments all can affect and gradually change your personality.

Sigmund Freud (1856–1939), the founder of psychoanalysis, is known for his many insights into the human mind—many of them still controversial. Freud believed that personality was established early in life and that personality disorders could be traced back to the traumas of childhood.

PERSONALITY DISORDERS DEFINED

The most recent edition of the *Diagnostic and Statistical Manual of Mental Disorders (DSM-IV)*, published in 1994 by the American Psychiatric Association, describes personality disorders as patterns of inner experience and behavior that deviate markedly from those experiences and behaviors characterizing most members of a given culture. Such patterns are pervasive and relatively inflexible. They can be traced back at least as far as adolescence or early adulthood, and they change little over time. These personality defects produce considerable distress and impairment for the individual who suffers from them. Family

Heredity or environment? Maybe both, say the experts. Personality disorders do run in families, but how this happens—whether parents pass these problems on genetically or similar experiences in the family cause similar problems in children—has been a matter of dispute.

members, friends, and other loved ones are often hurt as well—for example, by destructive behavior on the part of the individual with a personality disorder.

Personality disorders have an impact in at least two of the following areas: cognition (thought), affectivity (emotion), interpersonal relations, and impulse control. The patient might not consider some of the traits problematic, in which case the features are called "ego-syntonic."

There are two other important elements in the definition of personality disorders:

1. Only when personality traits are significant enough to hurt the individual and alarm the community are they labeled disorders. Someone with an obnoxious or troubling personality does not necessarily have a "disorder."

2. To be considered a personality disorder, defects cannot result from substance abuse, an independent medical condition (like a head injury), or exposure to a toxin. In any such case, a different diagnosis would be made.

Individuals with personality disorders exhibit exaggerations of character faults found in normal people. Therefore, studying these disorders sheds light on everyday problems faced by ordinary folks. Since all human behavior lies on a continuum ranging from mental health to mental illness, psychology is ultimately the study of ourselves.

TYPES OF PERSONALITY DISORDERS

The 10 distinct personality disorders identified by contemporary psychologists can be categorized by symptoms into three groups, or "clusters":

A. People suffering from *paranoid, schizoid,* and *schizotypal* disorders appear odd or eccentric because they distrust others and perceive reality in a distorted fashion.

B. Patients with *antisocial, borderline, histrionic,* and *narcissistic* personality disorders seem overly impulsive, emotional, or erratic.

C. Persons with *avoidant, dependent,* and *obsessive-compulsive* personality disorders are excessively anxious or fearful.

SIGNS OF A POTENTIAL PERSONALITY DISORDER

Because personality disorders are so varied, there is no single telltale signal that a person may be suffering from one. Sometimes the sign may be no more than an "ordinary" thought or feeling that becomes exaggerated. Nevertheless, certain aspects of a person's everyday thoughts, feelings, or behavior may provide a clue to a potential personality disorder.

For example, the on-line health guide OnHealth suggests that an individual should consult a doctor if he or she exhibits any of the following signs:

- Thoughts about suicide or self-harm
- Inability to have healthy relationships
- Constant trouble in keeping a job
- Frequent lying or trouble with the law
- Uncontrollable anger
- Continual feelings of inadequacy
- Tendency to avoid social interactions
- Inability to feel empathy for others
- Excessive craving for attention
- Fear of persecution
- Inability to trust others

Source: Adapted from OnHealth, "Personality Disorders," available at http://www.onhealth.com/

Although these different types of personality disorders have been defined separately according to distinct symptoms, many people suffer from more than one disorder or from features that typify different disorders. The other chapters in this book discuss the various types of disorders in turn.

Different disorders require different modes of treatment. In almost all cases, however, some form of professional counseling is helpful.

AGE, GENDER, AND TREATMENT

Personality disorders generally begin by early adulthood. Some can be traced back as far as childhood. However, a person younger than 18 years of age will usually not be diagnosed with a personality disorder unless the symptoms have been present for at least a year.

At the other end of the age spectrum, some disorders—notably anti-social and borderline disorders—tend to subside with age. Psychologists are not sure why. Perhaps the person improves with maturity, in response to changing hormones and other chemicals in the body, or perhaps environmental factors are responsible.

Some personality disorders appear to be related to gender. Borderline personality disorder occurs more often among women than among men. A number of other personality disorders, however—such as the antisocial and narcissistic types—are diagnosed more often in men than in women. Social stereotypes about gender roles probably contribute to the unequal distributions, but biological differences between the sexes may also be relevant.

The following chapters include discussions of treatment for specific disorders. The methods described vary with not only the type of disorder but also the needs of the individual patient. Generally, in determining a course of treatment, considering the relationship between mind and body is an important matter. Sometimes chemical imbalances contribute to moods, perceptions, or behavior that is counterproductive. In such cases, proper medication may improve how patients see the world and help them respond positively to their environment. For other persons, the best option may be individual or group psychotherapy—that is, "talk" therapy with a qualified psychiatrist or psychologist. Also, drug treatment and psychotherapy are often combined.

Distrust is a central trait of the paranoid personality. The paranoid person suspects colleagues and friends of disloyalty and betrayal and is prone to feelings of jealousy in love relationships.

PARANOID PERSONALITY DISORDER

W e often hear the term *paranoid* in common speech: "Oh, So-and-So's just acting paranoid. Don't pay any attention." Used in this way, the word usually means that the person is overly distrustful of others.

True paranoia is a well-known but rare disorder—a delusional system of thinking that results from internal causes (that is, the person's suspicion and distrust are not based on actual external circumstances) and that is reflected in the person's actions. It does involve a breakdown in trust, but one much more severe than that suggested by our everyday usage of the word. Etymology provides a clue to the disorder's seriousness: the word *paranoia* is formed from the Greek words *para*, which means "beside," and *nous*, meaning "thought" or "mind." People who are paranoid are literally "beside their mind" or "out of their mind."

Nevertheless, psychologists make careful distinctions about the intensity of a person's paranoia. Paranoid personality disorder, which does not involve such psychotic symptoms as delusions and hallucinations, is generally considered less extreme and disabling than either delusional disorder or the paranoid type of schizophrenia. Delusional disorder is characterized by a persistent "nonbizarre" delusion—a delusion involving a phenomenon that the person's culture could conceivably regard as plausible. The paranoid type of schizophrenia is characterized by very prominent delusions and often hallucinations. A delusion is defined as a false belief about external reality that a person holds to firmly despite clear evidence to the contrary. A hallucination is a condition in which a person has a sensory perception (usually involving sight, hearing, or smell) of something that is not actually present.

SYMPTOMS OF PARANOID PERSONALITY DISORDER

The person with paranoid personality disorder is quite suspicious of other people and often attributes malevolent intentions to them. The paranoid patient may think everyone else wants to exploit, deceive, or harm him or her even though there is no evidence of such intentions. People suffering from paranoia detect plots against them and fear attacks. They may believe they have been injured by friends or strangers, and they tend to see other persons as enemies.

Paranoid people are preoccupied with loyalty and trustworthiness, which they usually find lacking in their colleagues, subordinates, and bosses. Therefore, they constantly scrutinize the actions of others, looking for signs of betrayal. Jealousy is common with regard to sexual partners. Spouses, girlfriends, or boyfriends may be subject to constant challenges involving their whereabouts, affections, and fidelity.

Those suffering from paranoia are reluctant to confide in associates and often fear intimacy. They may avoid personal questions and detect hidden meanings where none exist. Others' honest mistakes can be taken as deliberate insults, and paranoid people frequently bear grudges and are unwilling to forgive. Such individuals are quick to counterattack and display anger in response to relatively trivial incidents.

In general, persons who are paranoid are difficult to get along with because they seem hostile, aloof, sarcastic, secretive, combative, or hypervigilant. Because they distrust other individuals, they often try to control everyone with whom they come into contact. They may be highly critical even though they don't accept criticism themselves. Such women and men tend to see everything in black and white; they are intolerant of ambiguities. Paranoid individuals may also develop negative stereotypes about others, sometimes in the form of ethnic or religious prejudice.

The fears of paranoid people may be counterbalanced by their grandiose fantasies, simplistic formulations about the nature of the world, and obsessions with power and rank. In response to stressful situations, those who are paranoid can experience brief psychotic episodes during which they lose contact with reality. Sometimes, paranoid personality disorder will evolve into schizophrenia, in which the person takes on the identity of another or is otherwise alienated from the real world.

Paranoid personality disorder should not be diagnosed if an individual is actually in a dangerous situation in which his or her fears are well-grounded in reality. For example, the ruler of Iraq, Saddam Hussein, is known to have injured or put to death relatives and close

Persons suffering from paranoid personality disorder have difficulty trusting others. Frequent outbursts of jealousy and mistrust can be very hard on any relationship, particularly a marriage.

associates whom he perceived as political rivals. Thus, a member of Saddam Hussein's extended family who worried a lot about his own safety would not necessarily be suffering from a personality disorder; he might simply be realistic.

A CASE STUDY

The following letter, written by a German woman who was a paranoid patient, was reproduced by Emil Kraepelin in his book *Manic-Depressive Insanity and Paranoia*. The woman was convinced she had been cheated out of an inheritance that was rightfully hers. Notice the wide extent of the conspiracy she imagined:

> During the fourteen years that I have lived here, I have led the life of a martyr which mocks at all comparison. It concerns the embezzlement of inherited money, and on account of this all imaginable evil and cunning was exercised, that I might be passed off as insane and so on, or that I should be made so, and that the necessary means of living, credit, and honor should be taken from me. This inexcusable behavior by day and by night is carried on by the secret police and their aiders and abettors, female and male, young or old, poor or rich—all must assist; since it is for the police! The hounding was ordered in all houses and districts of the town and no regard was had for an old widow full of years. Since I came to Munich, all my letters have been kept back, opened, and delivered without a stamp. Letters about inheritance were sharply suppressed, so that I never could be present at the distribution like the other heirs. Every effort is made that I may not be seen and that I should not come into contact with anyone; indeed it is horrible and incredible that such abominable occurrences can happen, carried out by certain lawyers, who have embezzled my money; of course they have also a certain police jurisdiction at hand, which facilitates for them their infernal ongoings in order that it should not come to light; besides they are rich, with which one can close the mouth of many a crime. . . . When I arrived in Munich I found my house in the greatest disorder, although, before I left home, I left everything punctiliously in order. The furniture was covered with a layer of dirt and dust, the bedclothes were thrown about anyhow, every drawer and cupboard was opened, although I had carefully locked up everything, closed the box of keys and taken it with me; in the kitchen the pretty mirror was in fragments. It went so far that I was forced to hesitate about eating anything, for after these rascally tricks people are capable of anything, whatever can be conceived horrible and mean.

Along with delusions of persecution, the woman expresses typical paranoid fears of contamination through poisoning. Delusions of grandeur (involving high descent or riches), pursuit by secret police, and hypochondriacal fears about sickness and health are also common. Memories of events that did not actually occur frequently upset paranoid people.

PREVALENCE AND TREATMENT

Within the general population, an estimated 0.5 to 2.5 percent of people suffer from paranoid personality disorder, males more commonly than females. Often it first appears in childhood or adolescence, when it may manifest itself as solitariness, poor relations with peers, social anxiety, hypersensitivity, underachievement in school, peculiar thoughts and language, or idiosyncratic fantasies.

Paranoid personality disorder occurs more commonly among families in which close relatives have chronic schizophrenia than in the general population. This suggests that heredity is important, but most psychol-

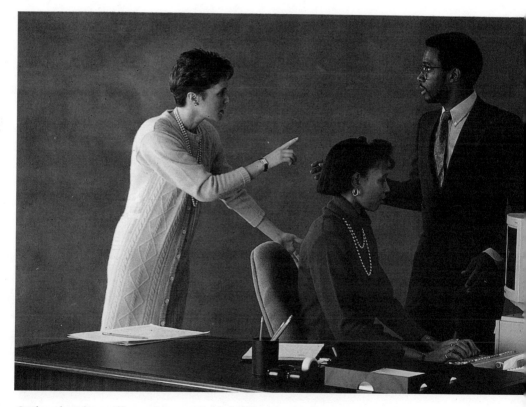

Getting along in an office environment is often difficult for the paranoid patient. Such workers would rather control their coworkers than cooperate with them.

Paranoid personality disorder often first appears during the teen years. Signs include poor relationships with peers, excessive mistrust of others, hypersensitivity, and unusual language or fantasies.

ogists also believe that the affected individual's upbringing and experience are significant factors in determining the onset of the illness.

Both psychotherapy and medication have been used to treat the disorder. Psychotherapy, however, has not been very successful in most cases. Even if patients are convinced that their fears are ill founded, they still *feel* distrustful. Nevertheless, being allowed to express suspicions in psychotherapy may at least take the edge off of the fears, giving patients a better chance of functioning well in the community.

Treatment with antipsychotic, antidepressant, or antianxiety drugs may help paranoid patients overcome some of the disorder's symptoms, even though psychologists do not fully understand the chemical nature of the problem. Paranoid persons undergoing drug therapy must be carefully monitored, however, because they may become suspicious of the treatment itself and begin to sabotage it—for instance, by merely pretending to take their medicine.

People suffering from schizotypal disorders may become preoccupied with "paranormal" phenomena. Here a man who claims to have been abducted by aliens displays drawings he made of the event.

3

SCHIZOID AND SCHIZOTYPAL PERSONALITY DISORDERS

L ike people with paranoid personality disorder, those who suffer from schizoid or schizotypal personality disorder often appear odd or eccentric. As discussed in chapter 1, these three disorders are categorized by the *DMV-IV* into Cluster A, which describes disorders in which people tend to distrust others and to perceive reality in a distorted fashion.

As the similarity of the terms indicates, the schizoid and schizotypal varieties are closely related. The *DSM-IV* distinguishes them in this way:

- Schizoid personality disorder is a pattern of detachment from social relationships and a restricted range of emotional expression.
- Schizotypal personality disorder is a pattern of acute discomfort in close relationships, cognitive or perceptual distortions, and eccentricities of behavior.

Neither of these conditions is the same as the psychosis called schizophrenia, which is more severe. (See the volume *Schizophrenia: Losing Touch with Reality* in the ENCYCLOPEDIA OF PSYCHOLOGICAL DISORDERS.) Generally there is a "spectrum" of disorders that show some elements of schizophrenia, ranging from mild forms like schizoid personality disorder to the most severe cases of full-blown schizophrenia. All of these disorders involve a failure to interact normally with other people, and some researchers believe that they are really different degrees of the same illness. Nevertheless, the currently accepted practice is to distinguish among them individually.

Another important point concerns the prefix *schizo*. As many people know, it derives from the Greek word meaning "split." But neither schizophrenia nor the personality disorders discussed in this chapter refer to what is commonly called a split personality. People with two or more distinct personalities suffer from multiple personality disorder, a rare disease not related to schizophrenia.

SCHIZOID PERSONALITY DISORDER

The detachment from social relationships that characterizes schizoid personality disorder usually begins by early adulthood. People with this condition don't develop close relationships and seem to derive no pleasure from being part of a family or other social group. The disorder may first appear in childhood as solitary behavior or underachievement in school that prompts teasing from other youngsters.

Sometimes called "loners," those with schizoid personality disorder prefer solitary hobbies. Mathematical games, mechanical tasks, abstract concepts, and computer work are more likely to appeal to schizoid personalities than are interactions with peers. Such individuals have little interest in sexual activities that involve other persons and usually experience reduced pleasure from sensory, bodily, and erotic activity. Walking on a beach at sunset or sharing confidences with friends would not be enjoyable for schizoid people.

Women and men suffering from schizoid personality disorder are usually oblivious to criticism and approval. Indifferent to what others think, they may appear withdrawn, socially inept, or self-absorbed. Such persons rarely reciprocate gestures or facial expressions and hence seem emotionally frozen. Anger and joy are expressed infrequently, if at all—even in response to provocation. Therefore, these individuals appear cold and aloof. The one strong emotion they may show is pain when forced into social situations.

Schizoid persons seem to have few goals and may drift through life. They usually don't date or marry. Occupationally, schizoid personalities are impaired at work by their inability to interact with coworkers. Most cannot enter into friendly banter with colleagues or otherwise cooperate in team efforts.

Schizoid personality disorder is more likely to manifest itself in people whose relatives have schizophrenia or schizotypal personality disorder. Slightly more males than females have been diagnosed with schizoid personality disorder. Overall, however, it is so rare that the *DSM-IV* considers it "uncommon in clinical settings," meaning that physicians seldom come across it. The *DSM-IV* also emphasizes that a tendency to seem solitary or emotionally frozen may derive not from a psychological disorder but from a person's circumstances—for instance, when someone moves to a new city or country and acts withdrawn or defensive in these unfamiliar surroundings.

The job performance of the schizoid person is often damaged by an inability to interact with coworkers.

SCHIZOTYPAL PERSONALITY DISORDER

Schizotypal personality disorder is more severe than schizoid disorder. Men and women suffering from the schizotypal form often experience cognitive and perceptual distortions. Their trouble in thinking and seeing like other people intensifies their desire to be alone and to avoid human interaction.

CHARACTERISTICS OF SCHIZOTYPAL DISORDER

In addition to having socialization difficulties, schizotypal individuals exhibit eccentric behavior in a variety of contexts. They may interpret life in unusual ways, assigning peculiar meaning to events.

THE SEARCH FOR EFFECTIVE MEDICATIONS

In the early 1950s a French surgeon named Henri Laborit was looking for a drug that might reduce the anxiety and shock that his patients experienced before surgery. He noticed that chlorpromazine, a drug that had been synthesized in 1950 by Paul Charpentier, fit the bill. Persons who were given chlorpromazine seemed calm about their surgery—even indifferent to it. Recognizing the psychological potential of this medication, Laborit recommended its use to psychiatrists. In 1952 two researchers reported to the French Société Medico-Psychologique that the drug was indeed effective for psychotic patients.

Soon the mental hospitals of France underwent a virtual revolution in treatment. With the aid of chlorpromazine (soon to become known by the brand name Thorazine), doctors were able to reduce the amount of restraint used on psychotic patients. Fewer institutionalized persons were isolated, and many ward doors were unlocked.

In 1954 the U.S. Food and Drug Administration approved chlorpromazine. By then, researchers were rapidly developing related drugs. An entire family of them, known as the phenothiazines, was soon available. Although these medications had significant side effects, they were relatively safe.

The phenothiazines are tranquilizing drugs that reduce tension and anxiety: they also change perception, attention, and mood. This group of medications became the first of the drugs known as antipsychotics. More recently, other families

Schizotypal persons are likely to be superstitious and preoccupied with paranormal phenomena outside the realm of their subculture. They may believe they possess special powers or can read other people's thoughts. For example, if a schizotypal young man thinks about taking the family dog for a walk but doesn't do so, and an hour later his sister takes the dog out, he may think that mental telepathy on his part caused his sister's actions. Some schizotypal patients believe in magic rituals—such as walking past a doorway three times before entering, in order to avoid becoming ill or coming to some other form of harm.

The way schizotypal people talk may be abnormal in phrasing or construction. Though this speech is usually intelligible, the sentences of antipsychotic medications have been developed. The newer drugs include haloperidol (Haldol), clozapine (Clozaril), and risperidone (Risperdal).

In the brain, antipsychotics affect the absorption of neurotransmitters—chemicals involved in relaying signals from one nerve cell to another. These chemicals include dopamine, serotonin, and a number of others. In certain types of mental illness, researchers believe, there is abnormal production or absorption of one or more neurotransmitters. Therefore, the right antipsychotic medication, in the right dosage, can make a profound difference in the patient's life.

Medical research continues, and each generation makes new observations and discoveries. Along with antipsychotics, classes of drugs known as antidepressants, antianxiety medications, mood stabilizers, and stimulants are now prescribed by psychiatrists. Therapists are becoming increasingly knowledgeable about the use of particular medications for certain disorders and clusters of symptoms. In schizotypal personality disorder, for example, antipsychotics in low doses are sometimes prescribed.

Still, however, the effectiveness of medication varies from one patient to another. What works for one person may not work for another, even if the two have the same diagnosis. Therapists need to evaluate each patient carefully to determine the right approach.

may be loose, digressive, or vague. A schizotypal person may also substitute words in odd ways, for instance, by saying that he or she is not "talkable" (rather than "talkative") at work.

The perceptual alterations symptomatic of a schizotypal patient may include hearing someone whispering his or her name when no other people are present. Paranoia can also be in evidence. In such cases, the schizotypal person might fear that fellow employees are secretly laughing at him or her.

Like schizoid people, schizotypal patients don't respond properly to interpersonal cues and seem stiff or rigid emotionally. They may avoid eye contact, appear unkempt, ignore social conventions, display unusual mannerisms, or dress inappropriately, wearing, for instance, ink-stained clothing that doesn't fit well.

As already mentioned, schizotypal individuals are uncomfortable with both acquaintances and strangers. At a dinner party, for example, people who are schizotypal do not become more relaxed as the evening wears on but are instead increasingly anxious and nervous. Tense and suspicious, they may become depressed as well. Transient psychotic episodes can occur if schizotypal patients are severely stressed for a long period. When admitted to a clinical setting, between 30 and 50 percent of schizotypal patients have also been found to be suffering from a major depressive disorder.

Approximately 3 percent of the population suffers from schizotypal

How "bizarre" one's beliefs are depends in large measure on the society in which one lives. These voodoo dolls, on display at a museum in New Orleans, are part of a religious tradition involving spells and a fear of evil forces—beliefs that in other cultures might be labeled signs of schizoid personality disorder.

personality disorder. It can first appear in childhood or adolescence as strange fantasies, social anxiety, hypersensitivity, or other odd behavior.

BELIEFS THAT MAY RESEMBLE SCHIZOTYPAL DISORDER

Sometimes people with seemingly bizarre beliefs are simply being true to their own culture or religion. In such cases, obviously, they should not be considered to have schizotypal personality disorder.

In some societies, for instance, the practices of vodun (also known as vodoun or voodoo) are similar to the magical thinking of schizotypal patients in our society. Adherents of vodun believe that if they stick needles into a doll, the person it represents will be injured in the places where the needles are inserted. Belief in shamanism (existence of a world of unseen ghosts), fear of the "evil eye," trust in a sixth sense, and other practices that Westerners might label "superstitious" are virtually indistinguishable from the ideas held by schizotypal patients. Similarly, some cultures require people to follow elaborate dietary rules and procedures to avoid ritual contamination; to a casual observer, the person performing these steps may appear to have a paranoid fear of being poisoned.

TREATMENT OF SCHIZOID AND SCHIZOTYPAL PERSONALITY DISORDERS

Patients suffering from either schizoid or schizotypal personality disorder may benefit from working with a therapist with whom they can establish an elemental form of identification. For the most part, however, psychotherapy alone has not proved effective in dealing either with these conditions or with full-blown schizophrenia. In some cases, medication may help bring the symptoms under control so that psychotherapy can assist the individual in rebuilding a normal life.

The pure schizoid patient may not have many symptoms that can be addressed with medication. However, antianxiety drugs may help such persons deal with the tension they often experience, and low-dose antipsychotics may reduce distorted thoughts and depression. With a careful choice of medication, many schizotypal patients can function well in the everyday world. Largely because of drug therapy, the length of hospital stays for such disorders has been greatly reduced over the past several decades.

Often called psychopaths or sociopaths, individuals with antisocial personality disorder show no respect for the rights—or at times even the lives—of others. Crime, arrest, and imprisonment are often the result.

4

ANTISOCIAL PERSONALITY DISORDER

A pervasive pattern of disregard for the rights and feelings of others, a symptom of antisocial personality disorder, usually begins in childhood or early adolescence. Yet in order for a diagnosis of antisocial personality disorder to be applied, the patient must be at least 18 years of age—with symptoms having been apparent since age 15.

In essence, people with this problem fail to conform to social norms connected with ethical, lawful behavior. Some people with antisocial personality disorder have been arrested repeatedly for harassing others, stealing, or pursuing other illegal activities. At various times this disorder has been termed psychopathy, sociopathy, and dyssocial personality disorder. Thus, a criminal labeled a "psychopath" by the media may, in clinical terms, be suffering from antisocial personality disorder.

It is important to realize, though, that not all criminals are mentally ill. Only when antisocial traits are inflexible, maladaptive, and persistent can a criminal be diagnosed with antisocial personality disorder. Conversely, a person with this condition does not necessarily become an outright criminal.

CHARACTERISTICS OF ANTISOCIAL PERSONALITY DISORDER

The typical hallmarks of antisocial personality include aggression toward people or animals and destruction of property. Antisocial patients are frequently involved in fights because they are irritable or aggressive. A reckless disregard for safety—one's own as well as others'—is often in evidence. In automobiles, these people may speed and drive while intoxicated, sometimes leading to a record of multiple accidents. High-risk sexual behavior and substance abuse may become chronic.

Individuals with antisocial disorder show little remorse or else provide superficial rationalizations for hurting or mistreating someone. To antisocial

One of the hallmarks of antisocial personality disorder is a disregard for the safety of oneself and others. Behind the wheel, such recklessness can have serious consequences.

patients, "Life is unfair" or "He had it coming" may be an adequate excuse for harmful behavior. Typically, such persons blame the victim for his fate or display complete indifference. They may be cynical about or contemptuous of other people's suffering.

Dishonesty is another consistent characteristic of people who have antisocial personality disorder. Their habitual lying can contribute to the need to make frequent changes in employment. Antisocial individuals often use aliases (alternative names), and as part of an effort to con other people they may lie about their education, past experience, and family background.

In their tendency to manipulate others, antisocial men and women share a characteristic with those who have borderline personality disorder, but with a crucial difference. In borderline personality disorder, the individual is deceitful to gain nurturance—that is, to get care and attention from others. In antisocial personality disorder, the goal is usually to obtain power, profit, or some form of material gratification. Some antisocial individuals engage in outright theft.

Behind their acts, such people tend to show a pattern of impulsivity—

that is, an inclination to do something right away without planning ahead. Decisions are often made on the spur of the moment without consideration for their consequences. Sudden changes in employment, residence, and relationships are common among antisocial patients.

Not surprisingly, men and women suffering from antisocial personality disorder are extremely irresponsible. This characteristic may be reflected in their significant periods of unemployment despite jobs being available. Absenteeism from work and school is common. Their financial irresponsibility may be expressed in writing bad checks, failing to provide child support or financial help for dependents, and defaulting on debts.

Attitudes of inflated self-perception, grandiosity, and arrogance are common. Antisocial patients may feel that ordinary work is beneath

Antisocial personality disorder is often associated with such impulse-control disorders as compulsive gambling. In recent years many state governments have legalized casino and riverboat gambling, giving pathological gamblers more outlets for their addiction.

them or that they are entitled to special treatment. Excessively opinion-ated, they fail to tolerate the views of others. Yet many of them can be articulate, poised, and superficially charming.

Antisocial people are often sexually exploitative. They may have a history of multiple sexual partners. Their aggressive and destructive behavior may also result in domestic abuse directed, for example, toward a spouse or children. As parents, they can fail to provide minimal hygiene, nutrition, medication, or care for their sons and daughters— who might depend on neighbors or relatives for food and shelter. Antisocial adults sometimes leave home without making provisions for caregivers to stay with their children and without leaving adequate money.

People with antisocial personality disorder may experience dysphoria (unhappiness), tension, and depression. Often they cannot tolerate boredom. This disorder has also been associated with anxiety, as well as with impulse-control disorders like pathological gambling.

Besides causing harm or trouble for others, men and women with antisocial personality disorder suffer painful consequences themselves. They are more likely than the rest of the population to die prematurely and violently—whether from suicide, homicide, or accidents. In addi-tion, they often receive dishonorable discharges from the armed ser-vices, flunk out of school, become homeless, or go to prison.

A CASE STUDY

In his classic book *In Cold Blood*, American author Truman Capote tells the story of Perry Smith and Richard Hickock, two men who in 1959 killed four members of a Kansas farm family they did not even know. The brutal murders were seemingly inexplicable. Both men were soon labeled psychopaths, and people wondered how the two could have become so antisocial. A brief look at Smith's background sheds light on some of the factors.

Perry Edward Smith was born on October 27, 1928, in Huntington, Elko County, Nevada. The following year, the family moved to Juneau, Alaska, where the father made bootleg alcohol. (This was during Prohibition, when the manufacture and sale of liquor were illegal.) There were four children in the Smith family, two girls and two boys.

Perry's parents quarreled quite a bit, and his mother began drinking heavily. Soon she was having affairs with other men, scarcely bothering to conceal her actions from the rest of the family. Later, while speaking to a psychiatrist, Perry recalled an incident when his mother had been "entertaining" some sailors while his father was away. His words were transcribed in *The Sociopath*, a book edited by Rita Bergman:

> When my father came home a fight ensued, and my father, after a violent struggle, threw the sailors out and proceeded to beat up my mother. I was frightfully scared, in fact all of us children were terrified. Crying. I was scared because I thought my father was going to hurt me, and also because he was beating my mother. I really didn't understand why he was beating her but I felt she must have done something dreadfully wrong.

Soon the violence began to involve young Perry more directly. While the family was living in Fort Bragg, California, Perry's older brother, Tex, was given a BB gun. Tex shot a hummingbird, after which he was very sorry. When Perry asked if he could fire the gun, Tex pushed him away, saying he was too small. Perry got angry, cried, and later that day retaliated. He picked up the gun, held it to his brother's ear, and yelled "Bang!" For this he got a beating from one of his parents.

Within a few years the elder Perrys split up, but the pattern of domestic instability and substance abuse continued:

> In Frisco I was continuously in trouble. I had started to run around with a gang, all of which were older than myself. My mother was always drunk, never in a fit condition to properly provide and care for us. I [would] run as free and wild as a coyote. There was no rule or discipline, or anyone to show me right from wrong. I came and went as I pleased—until my first encounter with trouble. I was in and out of detention homes many many times for running away from home and stealing.

Soon Perry was sent to various foster homes; in one, he got in trouble for bed-wetting, which is often a sign of underlying psychological problems:

> I remember one place I was sent to. I had weak kidneys and wet the bed every night. This was very humiliating to me, but I couldn't control myself. I was very seriously beaten by the cottage mistress, who had called me names and made fun of me in front of all the boys. She used to come around at all hours of the night to see if I wet the bed. She would throw back the covers and furiously beat me with a large metal belt—pull me out of bed by my hair and drag me to the bathroom and throw me in the tub and turn the cold water on and tell me to wash myself and the sheets. Every night was a nightmare. . . . She was later discharged from her job. But this

Robert Blake appeared as Perry Smith in the film adaptation of Truman Capote's In Cold Blood. *In 1959 Smith and his accomplice Richard Hickock murdered a farm family in Kansas. This savage and seemingly inexplicable crime shocked the country.*

never changed my mind about her and what I wished I could have done to her and all the people who made fun of me.

In 1948, at 20 years of age, Perry entered the army. A recruiting officer helped him by giving him a higher score on his qualifying test than he had actually earned. Rather than reacting with gratitude, Perry began to realize the importance of education and became furious that he had been denied it:

This only added to the hatred and bitterness I held for others. I began to get into fights. I threw a Japanese policeman off a bridge into the water. I was court-marshaled for demolishing a Japanese cafe. I was court-marshaled again in Kyoto, Japan, for stealing a Japanese taxicab. I was in the Army almost four years. I had many violent outbursts of anger while I served time in Japan and Korea.

Shortly after his discharge from the service, a motorcycle accident left Perry with lingering injuries. In Phillipsburg, Kansas, he was then convicted of a burglary he had committed and given a substantial prison term:

> I was sentenced to five to ten years for grand larceny, burglary, and jailbreak. I felt I was very unjustly dealt with, I became very bitter while I was in prison.

As these incidents from his life demonstrate, Perry Smith was exposed to domestic abuse and instability at a young age. From childhood on he displayed little empathy for others—even family members. Gangs, stealing, and anger at authority figures served as outlets for the boy's pent-up rage. The next section of this chapter discusses how typical some of these factors may be among people diagnosed with antisocial personality disorder.

PREVALENCE, CONTRIBUTING FACTORS, AND TREATMENT

According to the *DSM-IV,* about 3 percent of men and 1 percent of women suffer from antisocial personality disorder. In clinical settings such as psychiatric hospitals and outpatient mental health clinics, the rate can run as high as 30 percent of the sampled population. In forensic settings, such as prisons or substance-abuse treatment facilities, the percentage is naturally even higher.

Why, we might ask, is antisocial personality disorder so much more common in men than in women? Perhaps this difference stems from the diagnostic emphasis on aggressive behavior, typically a characteristic of males rather than females in our society. But some researchers have suggested that the disorder may be underdiagnosed in women—meaning that it may often be missed or mislabeled when it appears in females.

Low socioeconomic status—as was the case in Perry Smith's family—and urban settings are characteristics often associated with antisocial personality disorder. Again, though, concerns have been raised that the diagnosis may be biased. Critics say that doctors are less likely to recognize antisocial behavior among prosperous people who have considerable prestige and power. In fact, therapists have warned that a clever psychopath can fool the most sensitive psychologist. Masterful actors, such patients may have a lifetime of experience in charming and deceiving unwary victims.

HEREDITY AND ENVIRONMENT

Studies of adopted children have proved that both genetics and upbringing influence the development of antisocial personality. Because adopted as well as biological children of antisocial parents run an increased risk of having this disorder, it cannot be blamed on either heredity or environment alone.

Largely because of the genetic component, antisocial personality disorder occurs more often among close relatives of people who have the disease. (Female family members are at an even greater risk than males.) Biological relatives of individuals with this problem are also more likely to develop substance-abuse disorders and somaticization—medical symptoms related to psychological ills.

The influence of environment is evident in studies of children diagnosed with conduct disorder before age 10. Conduct disorder is a pattern of violating basic social rules or the rights of others, typically by

Antisocial personality disorder is found more often among the poor than the wealthy—but most likely the diagnosis tends to be biased. Psychologists may be disposed to recognize antisocial behavior in people who have not achieved the outward appearance of success.

aggression, destruction of property, deceitfulness, or theft (clearly true of Perry Smith). And since it includes many of the same behaviors as antisocial personality disorder, conduct disorder is often a prelude to the adult condition. Yet not all young people with conduct disorder go on to develop antisocial personalities, and the difference can sometimes be traced to their family environment. Unstable or erratic parenting, child abuse or neglect, and inconsistent discipline—all of which were evident in Perry Smith's case—increase the likelihood that a child with conduct disorder will become an antisocial adult.

Basic cultural influences are probably important as well. In the past, when more people remained in the locales where they grew up, and both family and community bonds were stronger, some potentially pathological individuals may have been prevented from following their antisocial inclinations by authority figures or community pressure. Today, however, in our highly mobile society, where individual account-ability to family, community, and moral and religious standards has been diminished, there may be fewer restraints.

For example, in relatively anonymous urban settings with transient populations, it is easier to act out negative impulses without the inter-vention of caring community members. Likewise, a deceitful existence is easier to maintain when a person can move on every few years. Such cultural factors do not "cause" antisocial personality, but they may con-tribute to its manifestations in everyday life.

TREATMENT

People with antisocial personality disorder do not respond well to treatment. Sometimes group therapy can help, especially in a residential setting such as a halfway house, but the dropout rate tends to be high. Medication is useful mainly in reducing associated symptoms like anxi-ety and depression and in controlling the most violent outbursts of anger.

Many times, when a person with antisocial personality disorder receives treatment, he or she has been forced to do so by the courts or by family members. Such involuntary therapy has even less chance of suc-cess.

Luckily, as the person grows older, the disorder—or at least its most extreme manifestations—often begins to subside. After age 40, criminal offenses become markedly less common.

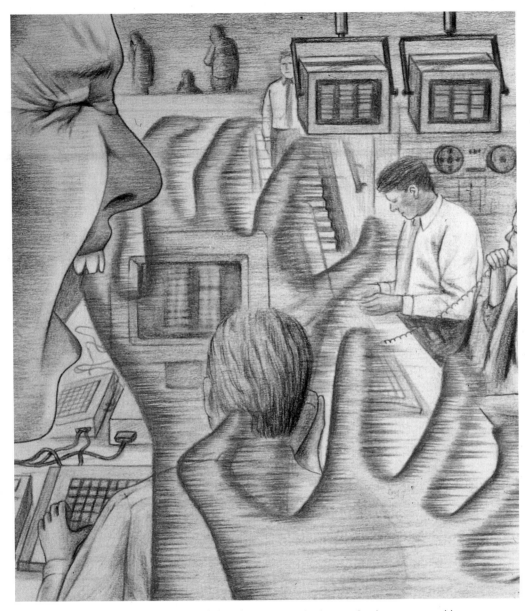

In the borderline personality, fear of abandonment or rejection can lead to unreasonable demands, panic attacks, and bursts of anger.

5

BORDERLINE PERSONALITY DISORDER

The term *borderline,* as used to describe a type of personality disorder, was originally chosen to signify that the patients were considered to be on the border between neurosis and psychosis. Sigmund Freud had used the word *neurotic* to denote less serious forms of mental disorder, troublesome to the individual but not entirely debilitating. By contrast, *psychotic* symptoms—like those present in schizophrenia—are more extreme. Although the neurosis-psychosis distinction is no longer so greatly emphasized by medical professionals, the term *borderline* remains in use.

People with borderline personality disorder are deeply afraid of being abandoned by others—loved ones, friends, family. They make frantic attempts to avoid real or imagined abandonment. The perception of impending separation or rejection can lead to profound changes in self-image, cognition, and affect (emotion). Borderline patients may react with unwarranted panic and anger, for example, if someone important to them is just a few minutes late or cancels an appointment. Intolerance of being alone can lead to self-mutilation or suicidal acts. A pattern of unstable, intense relationships often accompanies the disorder.

When they first meet a new person, individuals with borderline personalities may idealize him or her as a potential friend, caregiver, or lover. They may be overly quick to share intimate details about their lives with virtual strangers. But when the new person falls short of the patient's unrealistic expectations, anger and demanding behavior set in. The borderline personality may alternate between brittle, vulnerable, clinging behavior and irrational outbursts of rage. Intense anger may erupt in the form of sarcasm, bitterness, or verbal attacks, especially when the woman or man feels neglected or on the verge of being abandoned. Feelings of shame and guilt frequently follow these emotional explosions.

Emotional instability can also be seen in extreme mood swings—periods of intense irritability, dysphoria (the opposite of euphoria), and anxiety that usually last for hours. Likewise, periods of panic and despair can interrupt daily life because such people react so strongly to stress.

Borderline patients have an unstable self-image that may change dramatically. Usually they think of themselves as essentially evil, but this assessment can change without warning. Their goals, values, and occupational aspirations can shift quickly and often. Sudden changes in opinions, plans, sexual identity, and friends are also common. Such individuals often feel that their lives have no meaning and that they

The borderline personality forms unrealistic expectations of friends and even casual acquaintances, then often explodes with rage when those expectations are not met.

can't sustain relationships. They may be troubled by feelings of empti-ness. They may have particular difficulty in work or school situations that are relatively unstructured.

Borderline patients tend to be impulsive: they may spend money irresponsibly, gamble, drive recklessly, abuse psychoactive substances, or go on eating binges. Easily bored, they constantly seek new things to do. They often take risks.

Some of the behavior of borderline individuals is clearly self-damaging. For instance, they have a tendency to spoil their own good fortune or accomplishments at the last moment—skipping graduation, poisoning relationships just at the point when they have become strong enough to last, or sabotaging successes at work. Worse, self-mutilation (by cutting or burning) and recurrent suicidal behavior are major problems. Between 8 and 10 percent of these patients actually kill themselves. In other cases, lasting physical handicaps result from self-inflicted abuse or failed suicide attempts. The self-destructive acts are often prompted by others' threats of separation and rejection or by an expectation that the borderline person must assume greater respon-sibility.

PSYCHOLOGICAL DEFENSE MECHANISMS IN BORDERLINE PATIENTS

Sometimes the parent of a borderline person is also suffering from this disorder. In such a case, Freudian theorists believe, the parent passes on to the child the anxiety that she or he is experiencing. For example, a mother who worries irrationally that her son will reject her may protect herself by withdrawing emotionally. The unavailability of his mother causes the child to become even more needy. To defend him-self from fear of abandonment, the son learns to withdraw, too.

In addition to emotional withdrawal, another defense mechanism used by the borderline patient is *splitting*. In this situation, the caring, loving, "good" parent separates—within the child's mind—from the "bad" parent, who is considered harsh, remote, and rejecting. Similarly, the patient learns to separate his "good" self from his "bad" self, and these two sources of identity become ever more distant from one an-other. The "part objects" (good and bad) substitute psychologically for the whole person, who has both strengths and flaws. The idealized self and the idealized parent then stand in stark contrast to those villainous

The relationship between parents and children has been the focus of psychologists studying the borderline personality. In one theory, a child may respond to a parent's anxieties by becoming emotionally needy or withdrawn. In another, a parent splits—in the child's mind—into separate personalities, one good, one bad. The child then makes a similar split in his or her own personality.

characters, the bad self and the bad parent, who seem to have no redeeming qualities.

This delusional way of seeing the world becomes a habit employed to defend the patient from disappointment and rejection. However, this defense actually sets up the borderline person for repeated disillusionment. As new people come into his life, the individual first worships them as perfect and then, when they prove to have flaws, rejects and devalues them. At the same time, self-improvement is impossible because the patient's own self is split; that is, significant portions of his personality are not recognized by or accessible to him.

Typically, the borderline patient has other defense mechanisms that obscure reality:

- Avoidance, in which disturbing issues or people are not acknowledged
- Denial, in which the patient fails to confront the truth
- Acting out, in which destructive behavior replaces discussion
- Projection, in which one's own feelings are attributed to another person (so they can be dealt with at a distance, since such emotions aren't recognized within the self)
- Interjection (the opposite of projection), in which one takes characteristics from the external world into the self (this may involve an identity disturbance characterized by a persistently unstable self-image)

Some borderline patients fear *engulfment* (feeling trapped in a relationship) as well as abandonment. Others feel they must abandon loved ones emotionally lest they be abandoned themselves. Sometimes these individuals try to gain power over traumatic incidents remembered from early life—times when their parents deserted them at critical junctures, for instance—by deserting other people decades later.

A CASE STUDY

Fred, a 20-year-old, had dropped out of college because of severe depression and an inability to complete his work. His case is described by James Masterson in *The Narcissistic and Borderline Disorders.*

The third of three children, Fred could remember little about his upbringing before age 11. He did say that his family was fragmented: his mother and father were rarely home at the same time, and family members didn't do things together as a unit.

Early in life, Fred "obeyed" his mother and stopped seeing friends when Mom became angry that he was spending too much time away from home. But problems between Fred and his mother started in earnest when Fred began dating. Fred's mother was a domineering woman who never admitted she was wrong. His father, a successful businessman who worked much of the time, was passive at home.

Fred's sister, eight years his senior, was also in psychotherapy for severe problems. She had not been able to develop a career of her own or sustain relationships with men. The following account by Fred highlights his difficulties as he saw them:

> Life had no meaning for me. I suddenly realized that I had no motivation to study: I began to wonder why I was at school. Was it just because I was conditioned to go? I had no goals. . . . I looked at myself even more deeply, realizing I was so sensitive that I considered everything an insult. I tended to look at things from other people's points of view rather than my own.
>
> Even sex was not right. I could sleep with a girl, but it had no meaning for me except the physical release. I couldn't look a girl in the eye and be open with her. I'd never been able to be myself. I thought that the restrictions of the previous college had prevented me and that I could be more open, more myself at this new school, but I found out that I couldn't. I realized all of this, became terribly depressed and decided I could no longer go on.
>
> The more I thought about it, the more I realized the trouble went back to my junior year in high school when I first met a girl and began to have a lot of trouble with my mother, who objected to the girl. I also disliked the discipline at the [high] school. I lost my motivation to study and my marks went down. I knew I should leave; I became negative and angry. I began to cut classes. I had been captain of the tennis team and dropped out when I realized that I did it because I felt I owed it to everyone else and not for myself. I wanted treatment at that time, but my mother was against it. As a result, my marks were poor in my senior year, and since no good college accepted me, I had to take my last choice.

The psychiatrist handling the case recognized that Fred was suffering from abandonment depression and using the defense mechanisms of splitting and interjection. Splitting refers to the separation of various parts of the self (or others) from the rest of the individual's personality. For example, such a person may alternate between viewing him- or herself or others as entirely good or entirely bad. In this case, the young man had internalized the stereotyped images of his father as passive and his mother as aggressive. The "good Fred" would passively obey his mother's wishes and not leave home or become involved with other women. Once the "bad Fred" rebelled, he subconsciously punished himself by performing badly at school, withdrawing from situations that would promote relationships with girls, and doing poorly in other aspects of life.

Fred couldn't feel emotions that he thought his mother would not accept. Therefore, he couldn't relate emotionally to women. Fred didn't

Borderline individuals may be emotionally unstable and given to sudden and extreme mood swings. Their behavior is often self-defeating or even self-destructive.

allow himself to feel strong emotions, express himself, or pursue other interests lest his mother disapprove and abandon him emotionally.

The fact that his older sister was also suffering from borderline personality disorder lends credence to this diagnosis. Both children thought their mother would not accept them if they left home emotionally as well as physically and pursued their own dreams. Consequently, they didn't permit themselves real freedom or happiness.

PREVALENCE AND TREATMENT

Borderline personality disorder occurs in about 2 percent of the general population. It is much more common in women than in men: 75 percent of those affected are female. People who have close relatives with the disorder are five times more likely than the general population to be borderline themselves.

Among adolescents, episodes that resemble borderline disorder may appear, but they do not last. In general, this illness predominates in early adulthood and wanes with advancing age. The risk of suicide is higher among young adults than it is among older adults.

Treatment for borderline personality disorder typically includes some form of psychotherapy, which aims to help the patient come to terms with his or her subconscious processes and recognize repetitive behavior patterns. For someone like Fred, facing his fears of abandonment could help him prevent himself from acting in self-destructive ways. In this case, in fact, Fred and his sister might have been able to recover more quickly from depression if they had shared experiences and therapeutic insights, drawn strength from one another, and expressed bonds of affection that may have been inhibited in their home. In cases of this sort, joint counseling is often advisable in addition to individual therapy.

Medication is commonly used as well to treat borderline disorders. Even though a chemical imbalance may not have caused the problem, psychological troubles can produce physiological changes that need to be addressed independently. In cases where depression predominates, medications such as antidepressants, lithium carbonate, and low-dose antipsychotics may be useful. For persons overwhelmed with tension, antianxiety drugs may be prescribed. One difficulty with borderline patients, however, is that their symptoms can be so varied that choosing the right medication or combination of medications is difficult.

Even when psychotherapy is blended with medication, the treatment may need to continue for years. Hospital stays may be necessary during crises—for instance, when thoughts of suicide become strong, or when a relationship is near the breaking point.

The ancient Greeks were a sophisticated people who expressed their understanding of human psychology in terms of myth. Angering the gods by rejecting the affections of the nymph Echo, Narcissus was condemned to fall in love with his own image. Today his name provides an appropriate label for excessive self-regard.

6

HISTRIONIC AND NARCISSISTIC PERSONALITIES

L ike the antisocial and borderline patients discussed in chapters 4 and 5, men and women with histrionic and narcissistic personality disorders fall into what the *DSM-IV* calls Cluster B—that is, personality disorders in which individuals seem overly impulsive, emotional, or erratic. But histrionic and narcissistic personalities also share an intense and obvious craving for other people's attention or admiration. Let's look at each of these types in turn.

HISTRIONIC PERSONALITY DISORDER: EMOTIONAL SELF-DRAMATIZATION

Histrionic personality disorder is characterized by an attempt to draw attention to oneself, often through excessive emotion. This pattern of behavior begins by early adulthood. Since the amount of emotion typically expressed by a "normal" person varies from culture to culture, histrionic personality disorder must be evaluated according to the standards of the society in which it is found.

Histrionic patients are often characterized as overly theatrical. They are uncomfortable if they are not the center of attention. Lively and dramatic, such people may be flirtatious or provocative. If ignored, histrionic patients sometimes invent stories, create scenes, or do something else dramatic to call attention to themselves. Temper tantrums are not uncommon.

Histrionic individuals may embarrass their friends with public displays of affection, flattery, or elaborate gifts. Sometimes they embrace casual acquaintances with excessive ardor or sob uncontrollably over minor sentimental occasions. Such emotions can appear to be faked, because they are turned on and off so quickly. These people may also express strong opinions with dramatic flair even though their evidence supporting these positions is thin.

Patients suffering from the disorder often use their physical appearance to

"Histrionic" means theatrical, and people with histrionic personality disorder behave theatrically. They will go to extremes to call attention to themselves, often with extravagant displays of emotion.

draw attention to themselves. They are overly concerned with making an impression and may expend an excessive amount of time, energy, and money on clothing and grooming. They may "fish for compliments" or become inordinately upset by criticism or by photographs they consider unflattering.

Histrionic personalities are easily influenced by others. Highly suggestible, they may follow the latest fads. Overly trusting, especially of authority figures, they often turn to powerful people and expect them to solve personal problems. Histrionic patients may play hunches, quickly adopt conventions, or follow romantic flights of fantasy.

Such persons tend to represent casual acquaintances as though they are close friends. Although histrionic patients often behave in a sexually provocative way, they have difficulty achieving intimate relationships because they can't distinguish between true devotion and superficial association. They often act out roles, such as "victim" or "princess." Their interactions with others can show both manipulation and dependency. Often, friends are alienated by the histrionic person's need for constant attention.

Histrionic individuals become bored by routine activities and need novelty as a source of stimulation. Delayed gratification is particularly hard for them to accept. Long-term relationships are frequently neglected for new friends. Similarly, histrionic persons can become excited over a new job, but their enthusiasm and interest rapidly subside.

When people with histrionic personality disorder can't get the attention they crave, they may become depressed, and they are, in fact, at increased risk of suicide. Patients with this disorder may use threats of suicide to get attention, but these threats should never be dismissed as mere theatricality.

DISTINGUISHING HISTRIONIC PERSONALITY FROM SIMILAR DISORDERS

Histrionic personality disorder resembles several other psychological ailments, but there are distinguishing characteristics:

- *Borderline personality disorder:* Like histrionic personalities, borderline patients display attention-seeking, manipulative behavior, rapidly shifting emotions, and impulsivity. However, borderline individuals typically are also self-destructive, are disruptive of close relationships, report feelings of emptiness, and have identity disturbances not present in histrionic personalities.
- *Antisocial personality disorder:* These patients share the histrionic individual's tendencies toward impulsivity, superficiality, excitement seeking, seductiveness, and manipulation. However, antisocial patients manipulate to garner power, profit, and material gain, while histrionic personalities manipulate to win attention, friendship, and love. Histrionic patients are also more exaggerated in their emotional displays and usually do not engage in antisocial behavior.
- *Dependent personality disorder:* Men and women with this condition (discussed in chapter 7) share the excessive need

for praise and guidance typical of histrionic personalities, but they are not flamboyant or overly emotional like histrionic people.

Some symptoms of substance abuse and of other medical conditions can also mimic the features of histrionic personality disorder. With histrionic personalities, however, the cause cannot be traced to any external factor.

MENTAL ILLNESS OR CHARACTER QUIRKS?

Some of the traits describing histrionic personality disorder may remind you of the behavior of individuals you know. Many people, of course, have a tendency to be overly dramatic in some aspects of their lives. They may dress in attention-getting ways. They may often try to be "the life of the party." They may tend to exaggerate their stories in order to make their own lives seem more interesting.

Remember, though, that the mere demonstration of a collection of such behaviors doesn't qualify as a personality disorder. To be classified as a disorder, the traits must be, in the words of the *DSM-IV*, "inflexible, maladaptive, and persisting," and they must cause "significant functional impairment or subjective distress." A flamboyant, attention-seeking person who functions perfectly well in life is not psychologically ill— just annoying.

PREVALENCE AND TREATMENT

An estimated 2 to 3 percent of the general population suffers from histrionic personality disorder. It is probably equally common among men and women, though the way it is exhibited may vary, depending on the person's gender. For instance, a man with histrionic personality disorder may be given to incessant bragging about his golf score, while a woman may be more likely to dramatize herself by hugging everyone she meets and wearing the latest fashions.

The use of medication is uncommon in treating histrionic personality disorder. More likely, the patient will receive individual or group psychotherapy. Even though histrionic patients often have little skill at self-analysis, therapists can help these patients confront their tendency to manipulate others and help identify alternative ways for them to gain the reassurance they need. As with any personality disorder, if the patient threatens suicide, brief hospitalization may be required.

NARCISSISTIC PERSONALITY DISORDER: LOVING ONLY ONESELF

The essential feature of narcissistic personality disorder is a pervasive pattern of grandiosity—that is, an inflated sense of how important one is—along with a need for admiration and a lack of empathy for other people. The disorder typically begins by early adulthood, although some causes may be rooted in childhood experiences. Sigmund Freud started the psychological discussion of the disorder with his 1914 paper "On Narcissism." Subsequent thinkers—like Otto Kernberg, who developed the notion of pathological narcissism—refined and elaborated Freud's theories.

The disorder takes its name from Narcissus, who in Greek mythology was the son of a river god and a nymph. As a young man he was known for his beauty. However, when Narcissus rejected the love of the nymph Echo, the gods grew angry with him. They caused him to fall in love with his own reflection in the waters of a pool. Gazing at his beautiful and inaccessible image, Narcissus pined away—or, according to some versions of the myth, drowned when he fell into the water. The flower that bears his name sprang up where Narcissus died.

The contemporary period has sometimes been called the "age of narcissism." The individualism that we cherish, taken to its extreme, can become a deadly preoccupation with the self. Some thinkers believe that Western culture is especially prone to narcissism because it does little—compared, for instance, to Japanese culture—to teach a sense of modesty.

CHARACTERISTICS OF NARCISSISTIC PERSONALITIES

Narcissistic people tend to exaggerate their abilities and accomplishments, often appearing boastful or pretentious. They tend to talk endlessly about themselves and become annoyed if the topic of conversation turns to anyone else. Fantasies of unlimited power, beauty, wealth, or achievement may consume them.

Like histrionic women and men, those with narcissistic personality disorder crave attention. They, too, may exaggerate the depth of their interpersonal relationships, but they are more apt to stress their friends' high status or wealth. Narcissistic people want to be praised as superior, while histrionic personalities are willing to be viewed as passive, fragile, or dependent if this approach will help them get attention.

A LITERARY EXAMPLE OF NARCISSISM

Literature, drama, and film are replete with good examples of narcissists. In the great 19th-century novel *Anna Karenina*, Leo Tolstoy depicted two classic narcissists in Prince Stepan Arkadyevich Oblonsky, known as Stiva, and in the title character, Anna.

The 34-year-old Stiva struggles with injuries to his vanity caused in part by the aging process. (Narcissists sometimes have special difficulty adjusting to the limitations that come with age.) Stiva marries a woman named Dolly because she is a "good match" and because she has a habit of adoring and indulging him. However, after the marriage Stiva becomes jealous of the attention his wife showers on their son. Consequently, Stiva favors his daughter.

Soon the prince tries to find in mistresses the perfect love he no longer detects in his wife. He roams from one woman to the next, seeking perfection. When Dolly catches him in an affair with their French governess, he is unable to feel empathy for his wife's hurt. When first discovered, he even forgets to act concerned: his wife is dismayed that Stiva smiles blissfully rather than exhibiting consternation. The prince's habitual good humor is not clouded by the pain he causes those closest to him.

Later, Stiva feels sorry for *himself*—not his suffering wife—because he has to endure Dolly's anger. As Arnold Rothstein notes in *The Language of Psychosis*, in

In Anna Karenina, *Leo Tolstoy (1828–1910) created classic portraits of two narcissistic personalities.*

his discussion of Tolstoy's novel, "When Stiva's narcissistic defensive outlets are not immediately available, he feels no conscious inner sense of guilt. His chief concern is dealing with his disapproving wife." Stiva enjoys lavishing his money on elaborate, perfect dinners that are a reflection of his own sense of specialness. Every wine, entrée, and dessert must be unique. In general, the prince feels entitled to receive whatever he wants whenever he wants it.

Anna Karenina, Stiva's sister, is a stereotypical female narcissist. An extremely attractive woman, Anna is obsessed with in her own beauty. She always wants to be the center of attention and has difficulty yielding that position to anyone else, including her children.

Being ignored by an equally self-absorbed husband, Aleksey Aleksandrovich—for whom Anna is something of a trophy—is intolerable for her. She is enraged and humiliated by Aleksey's indifference and consequently makes fun of her husband. Like Stiva, Anna is unfaithful to her spouse and doesn't feel his anguish when he learns about her betrayal. In a fit of rage, Anna tells her husband that she loves another man, Vronsky, who pursues her with slavish adulation. As Rothstein says of Anna, "Her narcissistic rage derives from her own sense of entitlement. She feels she must be central to survive. Simultaneously, she feels entitled to pursue her goal. She is enraged at anyone who frustrates her wish."

Anna eventually leaves her husband and abandons her son. She continues trying to seduce other men—like Levin, who is happily married—and elicit their admiration. However, once Levin is out of the room, Anna stops thinking of him. Eventually, Vronsky tires of Anna, and she suspects him of being unfaithful to her.

In a dream Anna commits suicide because a peasant is taking no notice of her. Once awake, she soon decides that suicide is indeed the only answer. Through death, she hopes to reinsert herself into the center of Vronsky's consciousness. Rothstein concludes: "The tragedy of Anna—and of many narcissistic personality disorders—is that the quest for a perfect existence destroys her real life." She dies by throwing herself in front of a moving train.

Narcissists are routinely insensitive to the feelings and needs of others—telling former lovers, for example, about "the relationship of a lifetime" in which they have just become involved or boasting about their good health to a person who is sick. In the office or in other occupational settings, narcissists may expect employees to work very hard for

Are we living in an "age of narcissism"? Some analysts have blamed our society's frequent preoccupation with self on Western culture's emphasis on individualism and its failure to instill a sense of modesty.

them without taking into account the impact such sacrifice may have on the employees' family members.

Moreover, narcissistic persons are usually arrogant and patronizing toward individuals they consider inferior. They may feel they need to associate only with the most gifted geniuses who mirror the narcissist's own special status. They may refuse to consult with anyone but the "top" physicians, lawyers, accountants, hairdressers, and instructors. At the same time, narcissists are often jealous of the professional accomplishments of colleagues.

Such individuals may require great fanfare when greeted by friends and can become highly insulted if associates don't make a big enough fuss over their birthdays, promotions, anniversaries, or other occasions. Narcissists may be preoccupied with comparing themselves to others in areas like grades, salary, achievements, honors, or awards. Highly competitive, they may refuse to wait in line, fail to assist others in tasks they consider mundane, or demand special privileges for themselves. A sense of entitlement may lead them to believe that general rules don't apply to them.

Narcissists are often excessively ambitious and can react with rage or furious counterattack when criticized. Besides overestimating their own accomplishments, they often complain that they have not been afforded sufficient admiration. Typically, too, they are "bad sports" who don't lose graciously. Depression sets in whenever they sense defeat. Some narcissists withdraw when insulted or otherwise wounded and pout about their loss. They may feel unduly humiliated, empty, or upset in the face of rejection.

THE WOUNDED SUPERMAN

Despite the narcissist's grandiose pretensions, his or her self-esteem is usually quite fragile. A man suffering from the disorder may consider himself lavishly wealthy, an intellectual giant, or a legendary lover. However, the flip side of such a "superman" is a devalued self-image of helplessness and impotence. The narcissist has invented the superior self as a bulwark against the diminished self he secretly fears to be a more accurate representation of who he is.

Thus there is a split at the core of the narcissist's identity. The reason for inventing an overreaching, enormously inflated self-image is to compensate for the lesser self whom the narcissist regards with shame

The robes and flags of the Ku Klux Klan are universal symbols of hatred and intolerance. By projecting their own failures and insecurities onto other, hated groups, white supremacists may provide classic examples of narcissistic behavior.

and disdain. To support this attempted compensation, the narcissist manipulates other people into recognizing his or her grander self.

The "splitting" defense mechanism in the narcissistic personality is similar to that seen in the borderline patient. In his book *The Self-Seekers*, however, Richard Restak distinguishes between the two types of splitting. In borderline personality disorder, the inner split is more profound and, unlike the narcissistic personality disorder, it is accompanied by alienation and rage.

In his book *Shame*, Andrew Morrison cites shame and the need to hide—in order to protect the self from rejection—as the roots of narcissism. Feelings of inadequacy, inferiority, and incompetence are among the most difficult to tolerate, and the narcissistic individual tries to escape them by presenting a grandiose self and hiding the weaker self.

NARCISSISM AND PREJUDICE

Bigotry is sometimes fueled by narcissism because people who are "in love" with themselves can hate everyone else. In cases of racism and religious intolerance (such as anti-Semitism), as Bela Grunberger explains in *New Essays on Narcissism,* narcissists project onto the hated group all the qualities they despise, thereby ridding themselves of these attributes and leaving "pure" selves that they can love. The hated group can be any religious sect, race, minority, or nationality. Of course, the qualities that narcissists attribute to the group usually have nothing to do with the groups themselves.

PREVALENCE AND TREATMENT

Between 50 and 75 percent of the people who have narcissistic personality disorder are male. Overall, though, less than 1 percent of the general public is thought to suffer from this condition.

Many highly successful individuals display some features of narcissism, but this does not mean that these people have narcissistic personality disorder. As with other such conditions, the *DSM-IV* cautions that the disorder should be diagnosed only when the traits are persistent, inflexible, maladaptive, and cause functional impairment or subjective distress.

In therapy, "cracking the narcissistic shell," as Sheldon Bach puts it in his book *Narcissistic States and the Therapeutic Process,* is particularly difficult. Narcissists often don't acknowledge that they have any problems. Instead, they believe that everybody else is the source of whatever troubles they face. This attitude makes psychotherapy difficult because narcissists often refuse to see anything in themselves that they think needs to be changed.

Bach described a patient he treated who was able to marry after years of therapy but who admitted that he "had never really loved anyone" in his entire life. The man went on to describe the guilt he has felt over the years for having "murdered"—figuratively speaking—so many people in his life who had tried to love him. In an attempt to hide from this shame, the patient would fall asleep during therapy whenever the topic of love was raised.

In spite of difficulties such as these, psychotherapy is the preferred method for dealing with narcissism. Sometimes, family or group therapy can be beneficial since the narcissist's difficulties in dealing with others immediately become evident in this kind of setting. Ultimately, though, individual psychotherapy may be necessary to uncover childhood events or injuries that prompted such elaborate defenses.

The self-doubt and sense of inferiority that mark avoidant personality disorder may lead to with-drawal from work and social activities. By contrast, those suffering from dependent personality disorder may rely too heavily on others and may fear being alone.

7

AVOIDANT AND DEPENDENT PERSONALITY DISORDERS

Next we turn to Cluster C of the personality disorders—that is, ones in which the person is excessively anxious or fearful. As mentioned in chapter 1, this cluster includes avoidant, dependent, and obsessive-compulsive personality disorders. In this chapter we look at the first two of these, and then we consider the obsessive-compulsive type in chapter 8.

AVOIDANT PERSONALITY DISORDER

A general sense of inhibition, inadequacy, and hypersensitivity to criticism is the essence of avoidant personality disorder. The avoidant man or woman may withdraw from work or school activities for fear of rejection and criticism.

In marked contrast to the individual with histrionic personality disorder, the avoidant person is likely to be shy and to steer clear of any action that could call attention to him- or herself. Such individuals may be painfully quiet and seemingly "invisible." For people with avoidant personality disorder, intimacy with others is possible only after they have been assured of uncritical acceptance.

Basically, those suffering from avoidant personality disorder are convinced that they are inferior. They may believe that no matter what they say, others will consider it wrong. Consequently, they say nothing. These people can also be hypervigilant about the expressions and actions of persons with whom they come into contact. They may overreact, turning subtle cues of disagreement into mockery or derision. But their fearful or tense demeanor may itself elicit ridicule, which in turn fuels more self-doubts.

Individuals with avoidant personality disorder are reluctant to take risks or engage in new activities that could prove embarrassing. They may pass up opportunities for occupational advancement because it might entail new responsibilities. Avoidant patients tend to exaggerate potential dangers in

DIAGNOSTIC CRITERIA

Although avoidant and dependent personality disorders share a number of characteristics—such as feelings of inadequacy, hypersensitivity to criticism, and a tremendous need for reassurance—they have different emphases. People with avoidant personality disorder are mainly concerned with not being subjected to humiliation or rejection. Those with dependent personality disorder desperately want others to take care of them.

According to the *DSM-IV* diagnostic criteria, a person with avoidant personality disorder demonstrates four or more of the following characteristics:

- Stays away from occupational activities that involve significant interpersonal contact, because of fears of criticism, disapproval, or rejection
- Is unwilling to get involved with people unless certain of being liked
- Shows restraint within intimate relationships because of the fear of being shamed or ridiculed
- Is preoccupied with being criticized or rejected in social settings
- Is inhibited in new interpersonal situations because of feelings of inadequacy
- Views him- or herself as socially inept, personally unappealing, or inferior to others
- Is unusually reluctant to take personal risks or to engage in any new activities because they may prove embarrassing

ordinary situations and to make lifestyle choices that serve their need for security and certainty. For example, a person with this disorder might cancel a job interview for fear of embarrassment because she or he is not wearing "the right clothing." Marginal physical symptoms like headache or stomachache can also be used as excuses to avoid new activities.

Not surprisingly, people with avoidant personality disorder generally lack an extensive social network to help them weather crises. They are often described as timid, lonely, or isolated. Despite a longing for social acceptance, they fear putting their welfare in the hands of others

By comparison, an individual with dependent personality disorder exhibits five or more of these characteristics:

- Has difficulty making everyday decisions without an excessive amount of advice and reassurance
- Needs others to assume responsibility for most major areas of his or her life
- Has difficulty expressing disagreement with others because of fear of loss of support or approval (this does not include *realistic* fears of retribution)
- Has difficulty initiating projects or doing things on his or her own (because of a lack of self-confidence in judgment or abilities, rather than a lack of motivation or energy)
- Goes to excessive lengths to obtain nurturance and support, to the point of volunteering to do things that are unpleasant
- Feels uncomfortable or helpless when alone because of exaggerated fears of being unable to care for him- or herself
- Urgently seeks another relationship as a source of care and support when a close relationship ends
- Is unrealistically preoccupied with fears of being left to take care of him- or

because of feelings of inadequacy. Their doubts about social competence and personal appeal are even greater when they are among strangers. Yet, because they desire affection, they may fantasize about ideal relationships.

Between 0.5 and 1 percent of the general population suffers from avoidant personality disorder, and it seems to be equally frequent in men and women. Various cultures have different expectations about how outgoing or diffident an individual of a certain age and gender should be, however, so this disorder must always be viewed within its social context.

Many children and adolescents exhibit some types of avoidant behavior. But when such behavior worsens in early adulthood, the person may be suffering from avoidant personality disorder.

Avoidant behavior can begin as early as infancy or childhood with undue shyness and fear of strangers or new situations. Yet a diagnosis of avoidant personality disorder is not usually made for children or adolescents because a temporary lack of confidence could be developmentally appropriate. After all, periods of shyness or even withdrawal are not unusual when growing up. For some people, though, the avoidant tendencies may become worse during the teenage years and early adulthood. These are the individuals who may eventually be diagnosed with avoidant personality disorder.

DEPENDENT PERSONALITY DISORDER

The dependent man or woman has an excessive need for nurturance that leads to submissive, clinging behavior. People suffering from this disorder have trouble making everyday decisions and tend to be passive, allowing others to take the initiative and assume responsibility. Children with this disorder permit parents to choose their clothes, friends, and activities, while dependent adults may rely on spouses to run their lives. What to wear or whether to carry an umbrella may be an overwhelming decision for someone with dependent personality disorder. Such people require excessive reassurance, guidance, and advice.

Like those with avoidant personality disorder, dependent people have low self-esteem. Pessimism and self-doubt are common. They may belittle their own abilities. They feel uncomfortable when alone because of exaggerated fears that they can't care for themselves. They may "tag along" with important persons whom they greatly admire.

Since they do not feel capable of functioning adequately without the help of others, dependent individuals act in ways designed to get other persons to care for them. For instance, dependent people may seek out overly dominant types, who in turn need to control them. A small circle of friends whom they rely on excessively is typical.

Dependent patients fear losing support and approval. They may have trouble expressing disagreement with others, and they are easily swayed in their opinions. They may do things they know are wrong rather than risk criticism for objecting. With people they rely on for support, they seldom become angry, even when anger might be justified. Some dependent individuals endure mental or physical abuse and accept unnecessary self-sacrifice.

Dependent patients won't start working on tasks they believe others could probably do better. They present themselves as inept, even when they have enough ability to carry out a job. These women and men avoid responsibility, fearing they will be given chores they are unable to complete. They tend to evade challenges or tests. Consequently, they often don't learn the skills of independent living. Especially in an unstructured environment, they have difficulty acting independently.

If an important relationship ends, dependent personalities may be desperate to fill the void in their life and hence be too quick to find a

Effective treatment of avoidant and dependent personality disorders may involve group therapy, in which patients learn trust and acquire social skills.

new friend or lover. Because they fail to choose with enough care, the new relationship may turn out disastrously.

There is no firm evidence about the percentage of men and women who have dependent personality disorder. In mental health clinics, however, it is one of the most frequently reported personality disorders. It probably occurs at approximately the same rate in both sexes.

As with avoidant personality disorder, age and culture are important considerations. Obviously a young child can show much greater dependency than an adult without being considered mentally ill. Likewise, in some societies, girls and women may be expected to behave in ways that Westerners would consider overly polite and passive. If the behavior is typical of the society, it does not meet the standards for dependent personality disorder.

TREATMENT OF AVOIDANT AND DEPENDENT PERSONALITY DISORDERS

Various types of psychological counseling are the most common forms of therapy for these two conditions. For example, cognitive therapy (focusing on the individual's way of thinking) or behavioral therapy (focusing on the patient's patterns of behaving) can help the patient achieve greater assertiveness, better social skills, and increased ability to function independently. Joint therapy with family members can help affected individuals resolve their relational problems. Group sessions, in which a therapist works with a number of people who suffer the same disorder, can help patients build supportive relationships with others and help them practice their social skills.

In psychotherapy with avoidant personalities, a major goal is establishing enough rapport between patient and therapist that the patient can open up without excessive fear of criticism. In the case of dependent persons, the patient may seem on the surface more willing to interact, but at the same time may try to shift all responsibility for decisions and changes to the therapist.

Although medication is not generally used as a primary treatment for avoidant or dependent personality disorder, both disorders may occur in conjunction with other psychiatric conditions such as depression, panic disorder, anxiety disorders, and substance abuse. In these cases, the medication administered to treat the other problems may have an impact on the patient's dependent or avoidant behavior. For instance, benzodiazepines (the most popular kind of mild tranquilizer) and monoamine oxidase inhibitors (a kind of antidepressant) can reduce social phobia, a disorder that shares many characteristics with avoidant personality disorder. Generally, as other problems are brought under control, the patient becomes better able to cope with dependent or avoidant tendencies.

Excessive concern with order and neatness may be one manifestation of obsessive-compulsive personality disorder. People with this disorder feel uncomfortable when they are not in complete control of their environment and their lives.

8

OBSESSIVE-COMPULSIVE PERSONALITY DISORDER

Obsessive-compulsive personality disorder is marked by a preoccupation with neatness, orderliness, perfection, and control at the expense of flexibility and change. Painstaking attention to rules, trivial details, and schedules takes precedence over issues that most people would consider more important.

The words *obsessive* and *compulsive* are sometimes used interchangeably, but technically the difference between them reflects the distinction between mind and body. An obsession is an idea or thought that stays in a person's mind, while a compulsion is a type of behavior that a man or woman feels driven to perform.

There is another important distinction to be made. Even though they have almost the same name, *obsessive-compulsive personality disorder* should not be confused with the more serious anxiety condition termed *obsessive-compulsive disorder* (OCD). Someone suffering from OCD might have an incessant worry, for example, that her food is being poisoned—a thought that she simply can't drive out of her mind. Or an OCD patient might be unable to stop himself from performing certain rituals, such as washing his hands until they bleed or rechecking the front door hundreds of times to be sure it is locked. These are true obsessions and compulsions, and they are not characteristic of the personality disorder discussed in this chapter. In the strict sense, the person with obsessive-compulsive personality disorder does not have any one identifiable obsession or compulsion. Rather, the individual tends to be an utter perfectionist and "control freak," determined that things must be done precisely in a certain way.

Some people with obsessive-compulsive personality disorder become preoccupied with cleanliness. Extremely compulsive hand-washing, however, may be a sign of obsessive-compulsive disorder (OCD), a more serious problem.

CHARACTERISTICS OF OBSESSIVE-COMPULSIVE PERSONALITY DISORDER

In occupational settings, people with obsessive-compulsive personality disorder may be excessively devoted to their work—and not because of economic necessity. Rather, they tend to be workaholics, and they demand perfection from themselves and others. Obsessive-compulsives check endlessly for mistakes. When such a person misplaces a list of jobs to be done, he or she typically wastes much time searching for it rather than simply doing the things he or she remembers from the list. Finishing tasks is difficult for obsessive-compulsive personalities because they are never satisfied with the job. Consequently, they often miss deadlines.

When obsessive-compulsive people are at leisure, they frequently take work along with them so they "won't waste time." Such folks will repeatedly postpone vacations until they are canceled. At play, people of this type may turn entertainment into a chore—demanding that small children put colored rings onto a toy rod in the "correct" order, for instance, or turning music lessons into a strict ordeal. Obsessive-compulsives may require that all activities they engage in be organized. They prefer the framework of organized sports, for example, to aimless play.

Obsessive-compulsive men and women are unlikely to compromise; they remain rigid out of respect for their "principles." In general, these persons feel they must be in complete control at all times. They may dominate family members or employees. Such individuals don't like to delegate authority or share responsibility because they remain convinced that no one else does things as well as they. Typically, obsessive-compulsives believe there is only one way to do a job: theirs. They think there should be a set way to mow the lawn, wash dishes, or build a doghouse. Improvisation is annoying to them.

People with obsessive-compulsive personalities may not like to discard used objects or clothes "because you never know when you might need them." On the other hand, as part of a "cleaning" plan, they may give away or destroy whatever is not currently in use. Everything in the house must be "in its place." The children of one obsessive-compulsive mother complained that she gave away their winter clothes every summer. The husband joked that when he went to the bathroom in the night, he returned to find the bed made. Obsessive-compulsive individuals may keep their homes so clean that "you can eat off the floor."

On the job, obsessive-compulsive personalities demand perfection from themselves and others. They may react with anger and frustration when perfection isn't forthcoming.

Patients with this disorder tend to be stingy or hoard money, adopting a standard of living significantly below what they can afford. A wealthy person with this problem may worry obsessively about the price of lettuce or other mundane objects that he or she can easily afford. (Again, the person may object that "the principle of the thing" is what counts.)

Difficulty in making decisions is often a feature of obsessive-compulsive personality disorder. As a gag, friends of one such man gave him two types of umbrellas for his birthday, knowing that he would agonize over whether to carry the large, fancy umbrella or the small, folding one.

Obsessive-compulsive people are inordinately concerned with following rules or the law. Typically, they are submissive with authority figures they respect and belligerent toward sources of power they don't hold in high regard. They may be morally intolerant of any deviance from a single accepted pattern. In ethical matters they can show excess rigidity, which in turn can lead them to extreme self-criticism.

Obsessive-compulsive types can't usually express anger in constructive ways. For example, if a waiter offers poor service, an obsessive-compulsive individual is more likely to ruminate over the size of the tip than to speak with the manager. In fact, such persons tend to express all emotion in a stylized, stilted fashion. Frequently, they are uncomfortable around those who are more demonstrative in displaying affection. Everyday relationships have a formal, serious tone for most obsessive-compulsives. Greeting a person at an airport or train station, for instance, would include a smile rather than an embrace. Such people often object to public expressions of emotion. They try to control their own feelings as well as everyone else's.

Obsessive-compulsive personalities may become greatly agitated when forced to endure uncomfortable environments or wait in line. They can become extremely angry at any delay. Patience in passive situations is not likely to be one of their virtues.

CONTROL: THE METHOD
BEHIND THE MADNESS

The unifying theme beneath the cleanliness, orderliness, miserliness, indecisiveness, rigidity, and other features that characterize obsessive-compulsive personality disorder is the need for control. Some people with this condition suffered a traumatic loss in early life, such as the death of a parent or other loved one. Having been powerless to avert this past tragedy, the obsessive-compulsive person seeks to rule his or her present reality as much as possible. In other words, if the person can't dictate the big events, he or she can control the little ones. By doing so, the individual maintains some sense of a power to command his or her destiny.

In his book *The Obsessive Personality,* Leon Salzman claims that "obsessive-compulsive personality disorder is today's most prevalent neurotic character structure," in part because this disorder enables people "to achieve some illusion of safety and security in an uncertain world." Men and women who feel especially vulnerable—for whatever biological or experiential reasons—turn to "magical," irrational defenses against a confusing and troubling environment.

POSSIBLE BIOLOGICAL CAUSES: TWO CASE STUDIES

In 1996 Dan Stein and several coauthors published the results of a study funded in part by the National Institutes of Health. The researchers investigated the biological underpinnings of both compulsive and impulsive personality disorders. The following cases describe 2 of the 68 participants in the study.

MR. A.

Mr. A., a 48-year-old investment consultant, had persistent problems at work and at home. Having experienced depression throughout his life, Mr. A. reported that he had conflicts within his marriage and at the office. The patient admitted that he lost his temper three or four times a week, particularly when he felt helpless. Mr. A. described himself as "a coiled spring." During tantrums, he would smash plates and glasses. He also engaged in impulsive or thrill-seeking behavior that included promiscuous sexual relationships, financial risk taking, and deep-sea diving.

Mr. A. was easily preoccupied with small details and reported that he frequently wasted time and suffered from chronic feelings of emptiness and boredom. Because he felt that he always "had to be right," he was consequently indecisive. Mr. A had a habit of taking over other people's responsibilities in order to guarantee that things were done in the way he considered correct. His wife confirmed that her husband insisted on doing things in a particular way, whether or not the results were appropriate.

Mr. A. confessed that he had few spontaneous feelings, aside from anger, and that he had difficulty having a good time. He described himself as "moralistic" and was extremely critical of other people. "An eye for an eye" was one of his favorite precepts. A confirmed "hoarder," Mr. A. hated to throw anything away. He was diagnosed with obsessive-compulsive personality disorder.

MR. B.

Mr. B., a 37-year-old former lawyer, supported himself by working as an actor. Having suffered from numerous episodes of major depression in the past, he reported that he had ongoing career and relationship problems. The patient described himself as an irritable, moody person who made impulsive decisions without thinking through the consequences. From his rapid mood shifts to sudden professional changes, Mr. B. was a picture of instability. He had involved himself in intermittent gambling, shoplifting, reckless driving, sexual promiscuity, and the use of illegal drugs. As a child, he had often been truant, twice used a weapon in a fight, and stolen from his parents on a number of occasions.

Mr. B. liked doing things "his way" and often argued with his associates to convince them that he was right. In order to ensure that things were handled his way, he frequently took over other people's responsibilities. This perfectionism produced delays in projects as well as indecision: for Mr. B., details often obscured the big picture.

In describing his emotions, Mr. B indicated that he expressed his feelings in a "controlled and unemotional manner." He admitted that he usually neglected to take vacations from work. Something of a "pack rat," Mr. B. never threw things out. Like Mr. A., he was diagnosed with obsessive-compulsive personality disorder.

THE BIOLOGICAL SIMILARITIES

Despite the differences in age between Mr. A. and Mr. B., they resemble one another in a number of significant ways. And the study did not find just behavioral similarities between the two men; it also identified biochemical parallels.

The research indicated that these two compulsive individuals, along with the entire sample studied, have chemical differences in their neurotransmitters that distinguish them from the general population. Neurotransmitters convey signals between nerves. In this study, the biochemical differences observed among these subjects correlated with the number of compulsive traits exhibited in their lives.

The researchers focused in particular on the neurotransmitter serotonin, an organic compound found in the brain, bloodstream, and mucous membranes. It is active both in the transmission of nerve impulses and in vasoconstriction (the narrowing of blood vessels). As in other research on serotonin, described in the sidebar in chapter 3, this study strongly suggests that the patients' destructive behavior patterns are connected with abnormalities in their serotonin levels.

Much research remains to be done. We don't yet know, for instance, whether such biological differences are present at birth—although evi-

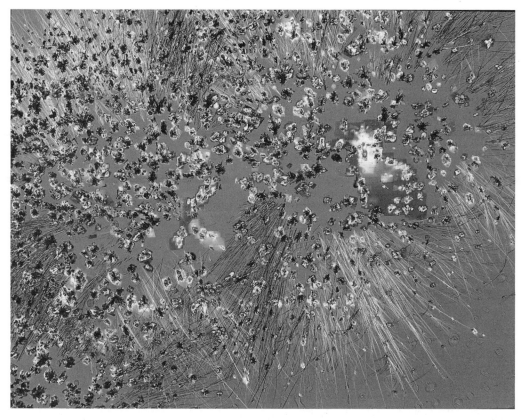

Shown here in a polarized light micrograph, serotonin is a neurotransmitter found in the vertebrate brain. Research suggests that drugs that affect levels of serotonin may be useful in the treatment of obsessive-compulsive personality disorder.

dence of the effect of heredity on this disorder points in that direction. Even if heredity is involved, do people's experiences also cause chemical changes in the brain? The interrelationship of mind and body is a fascinating aspect of current psychological research.

PREVALENCE AND TREATMENT

Estimates suggest that approximately 1 percent of the general population suffers from obsessive-compulsive personality disorder. It seems to occur about twice as often among men as among women.

Psychotherapy that focuses directly on the patient's rigid beliefs and inflexible behavior has frequently been helpful in treating obsessive-compulsive patients. For this disorder, the therapy is usually conducted one-on-one rather than in groups.

In some cases, use of medications has also been a help. Based on findings from the research on neurotransmitters, antipsychotic drugs are increasingly being studied for use with obsessive-compulsive personality disorder. Some reports suggest that antidepressants that affect serotonin levels are effective. When depression is one of the patient's symptoms, this kind of medication is definitely an option. Antianxiety drugs have also been used, but, because of the chronic nature of the disorder, physicians worry about the possibility of medication dependency.

As with all the other psychological disorders discussed in this book, each patient must be evaluated individually before a course of treatment can be determined. As Leon Salzman puts it in *The Obsessive Personality*, the goal is not to eliminate the *desire* for perfection, but rather to control the *need* for it. For men and women with obsessive-compulsive personalities, that is the difference between sickness and health.

APPENDIX

FOR MORE INFORMATION

American Academy of Child and Adolescent Psychiatry (AACAP)
3615 Wisconsin Avenue, NW
Washington, DC 20016-3007
(202) 966-7300
http://www.aacap.org/

American Psychiatric Association
1400 K Street, NW
Washington, DC 20005
(202) 682-6000
http://www.psych.org/

American Psychological Association
750 First Street, NE
Washington, DC 20002
(202) 336-5500
http://www.apa.org/

Canadian Mental Health Association (CMHA)
2160 Yonge Street
3rd Floor
Toronto, Ontario M4S 2Z3
Canada
(416) 484-7750
http://www.cmha.ca/

Knowledge Exchange Network (KEN)
Center for Mental Health Services
P.O. Box 42490
Washington, DC 20015
(800) 789-2647
E-mail: ken@mentalhealth.org
http://www.mentalhealth.org/

National Alliance for the Mentally Ill
200 North Glebe Road
Suite 1015
Arlington, VA 22203-3754
(703) 524-7600
(800) 950-6264
http://www.nami.org/

National Institute of Mental Health (NIMH)
NIMH Public Inquiries
6001 Executive Boulevard
Room 8184 MSC 9663
Bethesda, MD 20892-9663
(301) 443-4513
E-mail: nimhinfo@nih.gov
http://www.nimh.nih.gov/

National Mental Health Association
1021 Prince Street
Alexandria, VA 22314-2971
(703) 684-7722
(800) 969-6642
http://www.nmha.org/

APPENDIX

BIBLIOGRAPHY

American Psychiatric Association. *Diagnostic and Statistical Manual of Mental Disorders.* 4th ed. Washington, D.C.: American Psychiatric Press, 1994.

Bach, Sheldon. *Narcissistic States and the Therapeutic Process.* New York: Jason Aronson, 1985.

Banay, R. S. "Unconscious Sexual Motivation in Crime." *Medical Aspects of Human Sexuality* 3 (1969): 91–102.

Beech, H. R., ed. *Obsessional States.* London: Methuen, 1972.

Bergman, Rita E., ed. *The Sociopath: Selections in Anti-Social Behavior.* New York: Exposition Press, 1968.

Capote, Truman. *In Cold Blood: A True Account of a Multiple Murder and Its Consequences.* New York: Vintage, 1994 (1966).

Denny, M. Ray, ed. *Fear, Avoidance, and Phobias: A Fundamental Analysis.* Hillsdale, N.J.: Lawrence Erlbaum Associates, 1991.

Emmelkamp, Paul M. G. *Phobic and Obsessive-Compulsive Disorders: Theory, Research, and Practice.* New York: Plenum Press, 1982.

Fine, Reuben. *Narcissism, the Self, and Society.* New York: Columbia University Press, 1986.

Freeman, Thomas, John L. Cameron, and Andrew McGhie. *Chronic Schizophrenia.* New York: International Universities Press, 1965.

Fried, Yehuda, and Joseph Agassi. *Paranoia: A Study in Diagnosis.* Boston: D. Reidel Publishing, 1976.

Fulton, Mark, and George Winokur. "A Comparative Study of Paranoid and Schizoid Personality Disorders." *American Journal of Psychiatry* 150, no. 9 (1993): 1363–67.

Gabbard, Glen O., ed. *Treatments of Psychiatric Disorders.* 2nd ed. Washington, D.C.: American Psychiatric Press, 1995.

Gartner, Joseph, Sheldon Weintraub, and Gabrielle Carlson. "Childhood-Onset Psychosis: Evolution and Comorbidity." *American Journal of Psychiatry* 154, no. 2 (1997): 256-61.

Garza-Trevino, Enrique. "Neurobiological Factors in Aggressive Behavior." *Hospital Community Psychiatry* 45, no. 7 (1994): 690–99.

Grunberger, Bela. *New Essays on Narcissism.* London: Free Association Books, 1989.

Guttmacher, M. S. "Dangerous Offenders." *Crime and Delinquency* 9 (1963): 381–90.

Hoch, Paul H., and Joseph Zubin, eds. *Psychopathology of Schizophrenia.* New York: Grune.

Kernberg, Otto F. *Borderline Conditions and Pathological Narcissism.* New York: Jason Aronson, 1975.

Kraepelin, Emil. *Manic-Depressive Insanity and Paranoia.* New York: Arno Press, 1976.

March, John, and Henrietta Leonard. "Obsessive-Compulsive Disorder in Children and Adolescents: A Review of the Past Ten Years." *Journal of the American Academy of Child and Adolescent Psychiatry* 35, no. 10 (1996): 1265–73.

Masterson, James F. *The Narcissistic and Borderline Disorders: An Integrated Developmental Approach.* New York: Brunner/Mazel, 1981.

Medrano, Juan, and J. Angel Padierna. "Disappearance of Psychosis After Buspirone Treatment." *American Journal of Psychiatry* 153, no. 2 (1996): 293.

Mindus, Per, Steven Rasmussen, and Christer Lindquist. "Neurosurgical Treatment for Refractory Obsessive-Compulsive Disorder: Implications for Understanding Frontal Lobe Function." *Journal of Neuropsychiatry and Clinical Neurosciences,* 6, no. 4 (1994).

Morrison, Andrew P. *Shame: The Underside of Narcissism.* Hillsdale, N.J.: Analytic Press, 1989.

Murray, Megan, and R. Mark Newman. "Paroxetine for Treatment of Obsessive-Compulsive Disorder and Comorbid Stuttering" (letter to the editor). *American Journal of Psychiatry* 154, no. 7 (1997): 1037.

Paillere-Martinot et al. "Improvement of Some Schizophrenic Deficit Symptoms with Low Doses of Amisulpride." *American Journal of Psychiatry* 152, no. 1 (1995): 130–34.

Rapoport, Judith L. *The Boy Who Couldn't Stop Washing: The Experience and Treatment of Obsessive-Compulsive Disorder.* New York: E. P. Dutton, 1989.

Restak, Richard M. *The Self-Seekers.* New York: Doubleday, 1982.

Revitch, Eugene. "Sex Murder and the Potential Sex Murderer." *Diseases of the Nervous System* 26 (1965): 640–48.

Rey, Joseph, et al. "Continuities Between Psychiatric Disorders in Adolescents and Personality Disorders in Young Adults." *American Journal of Psychiatry* 152, no. 6 (1995): 895–900.

Romach, Myroslava, et al. "Clinical Aspects of Chronic Use of Alprazolam and Lorazepam." *American Journal of Psychiatry* 152, no. 8 (1995): 1161–67.

Ronningstam, Elsa, John Gunderson, and Michael Lyons. "Changes in Pathological Narcissism." *American Journal of Psychiatry* 152, no. 2 (1995): 253–57.

Rosenbaum, Bent, and Harly Sonne. *The Language of Psychosis.* New York: New York University Press, 1986.

Rothstein, Arnold. *The Narcissistic Pursuit of Perfection.* New York: International Universities Press, 1980.

Salzman, Leon. *The Obsessive Personality: Origins, Dynamics, and Therapy.* New York: Science House, 1968.

Samuels, Jack, et al. "DSM-III Personality Disorders in the Community." *American Journal of Psychiatry* 151, no. 7 (1994): 1055–62.

Sandler, Joseph, Ethel Person, and Peter Fonagy, eds. *Freud's "On Narcissism": An Introduction.* New Haven, Conn.: Yale University Press, 1991.

Schlesinger, Louis B., and Eugene Revitch, eds. *Sexual Dynamics of Anti-Social Behavior.* Springfield, Ill.: Charles C. Thomas, 1997.

Stein, Dan, et al. "Impulsivity and Serotonergic Function in Compulsive Personality Disorder." *Journal of Neuropsychiatry and Clinical Neurosciences* (Fall 1996).

Tolstoy, Leo. *Anna Karenina.* Trans. Constance Garnett. New York: Random House, 1965.

APPENDIX

FURTHER READING

American Psychiatric Association. *Diagnostic and Statistical Manual of Mental Disorders.* 4th ed. Washington, D.C.: American Psychiatric Press, 1994.

Bach, Sheldon. *Narcissistic States and the Therapeutic Process.* New York: Jason Aronson, 1985.

Carter, Rosalynn, with Susan K. Golant. *Helping Someone with Mental Illness.* New York: Times Books, 1999.

Kreisman, Jerold J., and Hal Straus. *I Hate You—Don't Leave Me: Understanding the Borderline Personality.* New York: Avon, 1991.

Mallinger, Allan E., and Jeannette Dewyze. *Too Perfect: When Being in Control Gets Out of Control.* New York: Fawcett, 1993.

Marsh, Diane T., Rex M. Dickens, and E. Fuller Torrey. *How to Cope with Mental Illness in Your Family: A Self-Care Guide for Siblings, Offspring, and Parents.* New York: Putnam, 1998.

Mason, Paul T., and Randi Kreger. *Stop Walking on Eggshells: Coping When Someone You Care About Has Borderline Personality Disorder.* Oakland, Calif.: New Harbinger, 1998.

Roukema, Richard. *What Every Patient, Family, Friend, and Caregiver Needs to Know About Psychiatry.* Washington, D.C.: American Psychiatric Press, 1998.

Simon, Robert I. *Bad Men Do What Good Men Dream: A Forensic Psychiatrist Illuminates the Darker Side of Human Behavior.* Washington, D.C.: American Psychiatric Press, 1995.

APPENDIX

GLOSSARY

Antipsychotics: a group of drugs often used to treat psychotic disorders. Although they are chemically diverse, these drugs typically work by affecting the action of certain neurotransmitters, such as dopamine and serotonin.

Antisocial personality disorder: a pervasive pattern of disregard for—and violation of—the rights of others.

Avoidant personality disorder: a pervasive pattern of social inhibition, feelings of inadequacy, and hypersensitivity to negative evaluation by others.

Borderline personality disorder: a pervasive pattern of instability of interpersonal relationships, self-image, and emotions, along with marked impulsivity.

Dependent personality disorder: a pervasive pattern of excessive need to be taken care of, leading to submissive and clinging behavior and fears of separation.

Histrionic personality disorder: a pervasive pattern of excessive emotionality and attention seeking.

Impulsivity: a tendency to act according to a sudden urge or impulse without planning ahead.

Narcissistic personality disorder: a pervasive pattern of grandiosity, need for admiration, and lack of empathy for other people.

Neurotransmitters: chemical substances that convey impulses between nerves, suspected by researchers to be keys to schizophrenia and other mental disorders.

Obsessive-compulsive personality disorder: a pervasive pattern of preoccupation with orderliness, perfection, and control of oneself and others at the expense of flexibility, openness, and efficiency.

Paranoid personality disorder: a pervasive pattern of distrust and suspicion of others, so that their motives are seen as malevolent.

Personality: enduring patterns of perceiving, relating to, and thinking about one's environment and one's self; essentially, the particular set of thoughts, feelings, and behaviors that makes a person who he or she is.

Personality disorders: persistent and pervasive patterns of inner experience and behavior that deviate markedly from the expectations of the individual's culture and cause significant distress or impaired functioning. These patterns can be traced back at least as far as adolescence or early adulthood. Personality disorders are commonly divided into Cluster A (paranoid, schizoid, and schizotypal), Cluster B (antisocial, borderline, histrionic, and narcissistic), and Cluster C (avoidant, dependent, and obsessive-compulsive).

Schizoid personality disorder: a pervasive pattern of detachment from social relationships, combined with a restricted range of emotional expression in interactions with other people.

Schizotypal personality disorder: a pervasive pattern of social and interpersonal deficits, including acute discomfort and reduced capacity for close relationships, cognitive or perceptual distortions, and eccentricities of behavior.

Splitting: a psychological defense mechanism in which the individual deals with emotional conflict by compartmentalizing positive and negative qualities into separate images of the self or of other people. The person's self-image, as well as his or her images of others, tends to alternate between polar opposites: for instance, loving, powerful, worthy, and kind versus bad, hateful, destructive, and worthless.

APPENDIX

INDEX

Anna Karenina (Tolstoy), 60–61
Antipsychotics, 24, 33, 52, 83
Antisocial personality disorder, 9,
    14
    and age, 16
    case study of, 38
    characteristics of, 35–38, 57
    contributing factors in, 41–43
    diagnosis of, 35
    and gender, 17, 41–42
    prevalence of, 41
    treatment of, 43
Anxiety disorder, 73
Avoidant personality disorder, 9, 14
    characteristics of, 67–70
    diagnosis of, 68–69
    and gender, 69
    prevalence of, 69
    and shyness, 68–69
    treatment of, 73

Bach, Sheldon, 65
Bergman, Rita, 39
Borderline personality disorder, 9,
    14
    and age, 16
    case study of, 49–52
    characteristics of, 45–47, 57
    and deceit, 36
    and gender, 16–17, 52
    prevalence of, 52
    psychological defense mecha-
        nisms in, 47, 49

and splitting, 64
    treatment of, 52–53

Capote, Truman, 38
Charpentier, Paul, 30
Conduct disorder, 42–43

Delusions, 19
Dependent personality disorder, 9,
    14
    characteristics of, 57–58,
        68–69, 71
    and gender, 71–72
    prevalence of, 71
    treatment of, 73
Depression
    and antisocial personality dis-
        order, 37
    and avoidant personality dis-
        order, 73
    and dependent personality dis-
        order, 73
    and histrionic personality dis-
        order, 57
    and narcissistic personality
        disorder, 63
    and obsessive-compulsive per-
        sonality disorder, 83
    and schizotypal personality
        disorder, 32
Drug therapy. *See* Medication
Dysphoria, 38

Freud, Sigmund, 11, 45, 59

Genetics. *See* Heredity
Grunberger, Bela, 64

Hallucinations, 19
Heredity
    and antisocial personality disorder, 42
    and schizoid personality disorder, 28
Hickock, Richard, 38–39
Histrionic personality disorder, 9, 14
    characteristics of, 55–57
    compared to other personality disorders, 57–58, 59, 67
    diagnosis of, 58
    and gender, 58
    prevalence of, 58
    treatment of, 58

Impulsivity, 36–37, 57
In Cold Blood (Capote), 38
Interjection, 49, 51

Kernberg, Otto, 59
Kraepelin, Emil, 21–22

Laborit, Henri, 30
Language of Psychosis, The (Rothstein), 60–61

Manic-Depressive Insanity and Paranoia (Kraepelin), 21–22
Masterson, James, 49
Medication
    and antisocial personality disorder, 43
    and avoidant personality disorder, 73

and borderline personality disorder, 52–53
and dependent personality disorder, 73
and histrionic personality disorder, 58
and obsessive-compulsive personality disorder, 83
and paranoid personality disorder, 24–25
and personality disorders, 9, 17, 30–31
and schizotypal personality disorder, 31, 33
Morrison, Andrew, 64
Multiple personality disorder, 27

Narcissistic and Borderline Disorders, The (Masterson), 49
Narcissistic personality disorder, 9, 14
    characteristics of, 55, 59, 61, 63
    diagnosis of, 65
    and gender, 17, 58
    and prejudice, 64–65
    prevalence of, 65
    and self-esteem, 63–64
    treatment of, 65
    and Western culture, 59
Narcissistic States and the Therapeutic Process (Bach), 65
Neurosis, 45
Neurotransmitters, 81, 83
New Essays on Narcissism (Grunberger), 65

Obsessive-compulsive disorder, 75
Obsessive-compulsive personality disorder, 9, 14
    case studies of, 80–81
    causes of, 81–82
    characteristics of, 75, 77–79

and control, 75, 79–80
and gender, 82
prevalence of, 82
treatment of, 82–83
Obsessive Personality, The (Salzman), 79, 83

Panic disorder, 73
Paranoia, 31
Paranoid personality disorder, 9,
14
case studies of, 21–23
in common speech, 19
and delusions, 19, 23
etymology of, 19
and gender, 23
and heredity, 23–24
prevalence of, 23
symptoms of, 19–21, 23
treatment of, 24–25
Personality, defined, 9, 11
Personality disorder
and age, 16
causes of, 11, 14
defined, 9, 12, 14
effects of, 12, 14
and gender, 16–17
signs of, 15
treatment of, 9, 17
types of, 9, 14
Psychopathy, 35
Psychosis, 45
Psychotherapy
and avoidant personality disorder, 73
and borderline personality disorder, 52, 53
and dependent personality disorder, 73
and narcissistic personality
disorder, 65
and obsessive-compulsive personality disorder, 82–83

and paranoid personality disorder, 24
and schizoid personality disorder, 33
and schizotypal personality
disorder, 33

Restak, Richard, 64
Rothstein, Arnold, 60–61

Salzman, Leon, 79, 83
Schizoid personality disorder, 9, 14,
31
defined, 27
and gender, 28
symptoms of, 28
treatment of, 33
Schizophrenia
and paranoid personality disorder, 20, 23
and personality disorders, 27
and psychotherapy, 33
Schizotypal personality disorder, 9,
14
characteristics of, 29, 31–32
and cultural beliefs and practices, 32–33
defined, 27
treatment of, 33
Self-Seekers, The (Restak), 64
Shame (Morrison), 64
Smith, Perry, 38–41, 43
Sociopath, The (Bergman), 39
Somaticization, 42
Split personality, 27
Splitting, 47, 51, 64
Stein, Dan, 80
Substance abuse, 14
and antisocial personality disorder, 42
and avoidant personality disorder, 73

and dependent personality disorder, 73
and histrionic personality disorder, 58
Suicide
and antisocial personality disorder, 37

and borderline personality disorder, 45, 47, 52, 53
and histrionic personality disorder, 57, 58

Tolstoy, Leo, 60–61